The Athenian Funeral Orations

The Focus Philosophical Library
Series Editor • Albert Keith Whitaker

The Athenian Funeral Orations

Translation, Introduction
and Notes

Judson Herrman
Bowdoin College

Focus Publishing
R. Pullins Co.
Newburyport, MA

Copyright © 2004 Judson Herrman

ISBN 1-58510-078-1

Cover: The Stele of Dexileos. Photo courtesy Prometheus Imports.

Book Team:
Publisher: Ron Pullins
Production Manager: Linda Robertson
Editorial Manager: Cynthia Zawalich

Printed in the United States of America
10   9   8   7   6   5   4   3   2   1

CONTENTS

Preface

This work has grown up as a side-project to my PhD dissertation, which consisted of a new edition and translation of the funeral orations of Demosthenes and Hyperides, accompanied by a literary and historical commentary (Harvard, 1999). I am very grateful to its director, Albert Henrichs, for his inspiring guidance and support. Thanks also to Stephen Esposito for specific comments and help and advice in planning the volume, and to Ron Pullins and Focus Publishing for their confidence in this project and the classics. I would also like to thank an anonymous reader for very helpful comments.

I would like to dedicate this book to the memory of my grandfather.

I. Context and content

Throughout the fifth and fourth centuries BC,[1] at the close of each campaign season the Athenian state honored its war-dead in a public burial ceremony, choosing a prominent orator to give the keynote address. This volume collects all of the surviving state funeral orations from classical Athens.

Like tragedy, these speeches present an image of an idealized Athens. The narratives of past Athenian glories found in these speeches feature many of the same mythical tales that were also presented on stage. Like many of the plays, the funeral orations emphasize important themes such as Athenian unity, their aid to suppliants, and their willingness to drive away foreign invaders to protect the other Greeks. The selective version of more recent history found in the funeral orations also highlights these same qualities by focusing on the role of Athens during the Persian Wars (490–479), when the city helped save the other Greeks from invading foreigners, and by passing over other events, such as the Peloponnesian War (431–404), in which Athens opposed fellow Greeks. Although nearly all of the surviving Greek tragedies are set in the distant mythical past (the significant exception is Aeschylus' *Persians*), the audience in the theater would recognize aspects of contemporary Athens in the depiction of ancient Athenian heroes such as Theseus. The funeral orations draw similar connections more explicitly by presenting a continuous narrative tying the present generation with the great heroes of long ago.

The fallen soldiers are linked with the Athenian heroes of the past and by sacrificing their lives for the state they achieve an almost divine status.[2] Whether rich or poor, a young man who dies in the field receives the same honors.[3] Prior to the institution of the public burial such honors were reserved for the upper class.[4] The orations glorify death on the battlefield as a private sacrifice for the public good.[5] They

---

[1] Aside from bibliographic references, all dates are BC unless otherwise indicated.

[2] In Greece the term 'hero' denotes a mortal human, usually from the distant past, who was worshiped with regular rites at a tomb site. Demosthenes (27–31) describes the Eponymous Heroes who were worshiped as heroes in Athens. The annual games for the dead and their public tomb were characteristic of hero worship.

[3] See glossary under **brave**.

[4] See p. 4 below.

[5] See glossary under **public and private**.

assign these honors collectively: individuals are rarely named.[6] Instead
the city is praised as the single entity responsible for all of the Athenians' past achievements. An American might point to the Bill of Rights
as a document that defines our national values (at least in theory if not
in practice), but the Athenians had no such official documents defining
their government. The descriptions of the city found in these orations
provide our clearest exposition of Athenian democratic ideology.

Before turning to these orations, let's consider their institutional
context. These speeches were delivered as part of a state burial ceremony. Most of our knowledge of the ceremony comes from the speeches
themselves, and especially from Thucydides' introduction to Pericles'
speech (2.34). The historian begins with the "laying out", or *prothe-
sis*, of the remains in coffins, one for each of the ten Athenian tribes.
This display is likely to have taken place in the marketplace, or *agora*,
of Athens, although none of our sources says as much. Next they hold
a formal procession, or *ekphora*, to the public cemetery, named the Ceramicus (which means "the potters' quarter"), located about a kilo-
meter northwest of the *agora*, just outside the city walls. There the
remains are placed in the public grave, or *dēmosion sēma*, and the funeral oration is delivered. After the speech there were competitions in
athletics, horse-racing and music for the dead.[7]

Thucydides also observes that this custom was celebrated
"throughout the entire war, whenever the occasion arose" (34.7).
Presumably the rites were observed annually whenever there were
Athenian war-dead to bury. Thucydides (34.1 and 47.1) dates the
ceremony to the winter, and it would have been reasonable for the
Athenians to gather together and lament the dead then, after the
campaign season had ended and the cremated remains of the dead
had been brought to Athens. Hyperides' speech, on the other hand,
refers to recent events at the beginning of the year 322, and must have
been delivered in spring, not winter. Although some have proposed
associating the burial with particular events on the Athenian festival
calendar, these differences probably indicate that there was no fixed
date for the ceremony.

The precise date of the introduction of the public burial as an institution is controversial, but it was probably in the 470s or 460s. Prior to
the introduction of the burial ceremony in Athens fallen soldiers were

---

[6] Hyperides' oration is quite unusual in this regard; see the introduction
to that work.

[7] Some sources say the games were held in the Ceramicus, others in the
agora (Pritchett 1985, 107 collects the references). The descriptions of
the games are very brief: see Lysias 80, Plato 249b and Demosthenes
13.

buried on the spot after battle.[8] The ancient travel-writer Pausanias, writing in the second century AD, linked the origin of the institution with the battle of Drabescus in 465/4, although he also refers to earlier Athenian state tombs in his description of the Ceramicus (1.29.4–14). As a result some have preferred an earlier date in the 470s, perhaps in connection with Cimon's recovery of the bones of Theseus in 475.[9] Others have argued for a later date on the basis of literary parallels and possible historical allusions to Athenian attitudes in the 460s.[10] In summary, our evidence for the original date of the institution is slight and contradictory, but the tradition of burying the dead in Athens probably began in the late 470s or early 460s.

Archaeological evidence also contributes to our knowledge of the public burial ceremony. Several Athenian casualty lists carved in stone survive, at least in part, from the fifth and fourth centuries.[11] These inscriptions typically refer to a particular battle location and then list the fallen Athenians individually by name under headings for each tribe.[12] These monumental inscriptions were put on display to remind the living of the sacrifice made by the dead for the Athenians.[13] In recent years remains from a number of mass-graves (*polyandreia*), which are believed to be part of the *dēmosion sēma*, have been discovered, containing bone remains from the time of the Peloponnesian War.[14]

Like the religious festivals that featured dramatic productions, the ceremony for the burial of the war dead was considered uniquely Athenian.[15] The Athenians were unusual in that they had a civic institution to celebrate the dead, and fallen soldiers from all walks of life were equally, and anonymously, honored. But the Greeks had long regarded death in battle as heroic and honorable. Book 23 of the *Iliad*, originally composed in the eighth century, features a narrative of the funeral games in honor of the Greek fighter Patroclus. Later, in the seventh

---

[8] See for example, Herodotus 9.85.2 on Plataea. Thucydides (2.34.5) observes that the burial of the dead in 490 at the battle-site in Marathon was designed as a special honor, although the practice was not uncommon at the time.

[9] On the bones of Theseus see Pausanias 3.3.7.

[10] Loraux 1986, 56–76

[11] For an example, see Fornara 1983, no. 78.

[12] On the tribal system see note 44 (p. 71) on Demosthenes.

[13] Tritle 2000, 165–183 discusses these inscriptions along with other monuments for the dead in Athens and Greece. He compares American monuments, ranging from the National Cemetery at Gettysburg to the Vietnam Memorial in Washington.

[14] See Rose 2000 for a preliminary report on the discovery.

[15] Demosthenes, *Against Leptines* 141: "you alone of all men make public funeral orations for the dead."

century, elegiac poets such as Tyrtaeus (from Sparta), Callinus (from Ephesus in Asia Minor), and Mimnermus (from Smyrna in Asia Minor) praised the glory of death in battle. In the sixth century elaborate grave markers, many with dedicatory verse inscriptions, honor fallen aristocrats.[16] And after the Persian Wars poets such as Simonides continued to celebrate the glory of soldiers who died in battle.[17] These accounts tend to praise *hoplite* warriors, who were soldiers wealthy enough to provide their own arms. The state funeral orations do not make such a pronounced class distinction, and rowers in the navy who were too poor to fight as *hoplites* receive the same honor as the richest cavalry soldiers.

The formal public burial ceremony of the war dead in Athens had its roots in these earlier attitudes and practices. Near the end of the sixth century (in 510), Cleisthenes came to power in Athens and implemented many democratic measures. For the previous half-century, while the tyrant Pisistratus and his son Hippias were in power in Athens (561–510), aristocratic factionalism was rife. Cleisthenes hoped to diminish the prominence of these aristocrats and his democratic reforms were probably responsible, at least in part, for the virtual disappearance of aristocratic grave markers at the end of the sixth century. After this, one plausible hypothesis suggests that a series of gradual steps may have led to the institution of the burial ceremony:[18] at first outstanding fallen soldiers, perhaps often of aristocratic background, were individually honored with some sort of 'public' burial on the battlefield; gradually all of the fallen soldiers after a battle came to be included in this honor and the dead were celebrated collectively and anonymously, not individually; at last, after the Persian Wars, the formal ceremony as we know it was instituted at the Ceramicus in Athens. The delivery of a oration may have been one of the later additions to the ceremony; we have no references to any speeches before 440/439, and one ancient critic refers to the lateness of this element of the ceremony.[19]

Now that we have considered the nature and history of the burial ceremony as an institution, let's focus on the funeral orations that were given at the burial. First, a summary of the six speeches included in this volume (for more details see the individual introductions to each item):

---

[16] On these graves see Morris 1992.

[17] On the Persian Wars see note 28 (p. 33) on Lysias. On Simonides see note 32 (p. 18) on Thucydides.

[18] Parker 1996, 134–135.

[19] Dionysius of Halicarnassus, *Roman Antiquities* 5.17.4. Compare also Thucydides 35.1: "added this speech ...."

- Speech delivered by the Athenian statesman Pericles in 431, rewritten by Thucydides and included in his *History of the Peloponnesian War*;

- Short fragments of a speech by the rhetorician Gorgias, from Leontini in Sicily, composed during the Peloponnesian War, probably for teaching purposes, not for actual delivery;

- Oration by the speechwriter Lysias, written in the late 390s, also not delivered;

- An oration embedded in Plato's dialogue *Menexenus*, written shortly after 386, which Socrates says he heard from Aspasia, the famous mistress of Pericles;

- A speech actually delivered by the politician Demosthenes after the Athenians were defeated at Chaeronea in 338;

- An oration by the politician Hyperides, also actually delivered, after the first season of the Lamian War in 322.

Aside from these speeches, we also have a few references to one other state funeral oration, earlier than all of those that survive, delivered by Pericles in 440/39. Of this speech we have only brief fragments, which include two striking conceits. Plutarch, a biographer active during the first and second century AD, provides a fragment of another historian's account of Pericles' speech: "Stesimbrotus says that, when he [Pericles] was praising those who died at Samos at their grave, he said that they had become immortal like the gods. 'For we do not see them, but from the honors they receive and the goods which they provide we infer that they are immortal.' He adds that the same thing is true of those who have died for their fatherland."[20] Aristotle, while discussing the subject of "the greater" and "the lesser," also preserves a brief quotation: "... just as Pericles says in the funeral oration that taking the youth from the city is like taking the Spring from the year."[21] Euripides' *Supplices*, a tragedy produced in Athens between 424 and 419, also contains a poetic account set in mythological time that clearly alludes to contemporary funeral orations in Athens (ll. 399–462). The influence of the genre can also be seen in the historian Herodotus' account (9.27) of an Athenian speech before the battle of Plataea that features many of the common themes of the state funeral orations.[22]

All of the surviving speeches display a common structure, and later rhetorical theorists refer to these same standard elements for funeral

---

[20] Plutarch, *Pericles* 8.9; compare 28.4–6.
[21] Aristotle, *Rhetoric* 1365a 32–33.
[22] On Plataea, see note 46 (p. 37) on Lysias.

orations.[23] Full speeches include (1) an introduction (*prooimion*), (2) a praise section (*epainos*), (3) consolation (*paramythia*), (4) conclusion (*epilogos*). The surviving speeches may be analyzed as follows:

	prooimion	epainos	paramythia	epilogos
Thuc.	35	36–42	43–45	46
Gorgias		5a–6		
Lysias	1–2	3–76	77–80	81
Plato	236d–237a	237b–246a	246b–249c	249c
Dem.	1–3	3–31	32–37	37
Hyp.	1–2	3–40	41–43	

The "praise," or *epainos* section of the speeches typically included a number of standard elements.[24] Orators might begin by praising the ancestors and family-line of the dead.[25] It was commonly asserted that the original Athenians were long ago born from the very land they lived in.[26] Because of this common origin the Athenians boasted that they were especially unified, and that their civilization was more advanced since they had been in one place longer than any other people. The Athenians were also proud of their local produce and orations often allude to the myth of Demeter.[27] Next, the orator's praise of the ancestors might refer to various honorable deeds, ranging from the mythological past to recent events.[28] The Athenians saved the other Greeks from foreign invaders, by fighting the Amazons and Eumolpus long ago in the time of myth,[29] and then by defeating the Persians and fighting the Macedonians.[30] The Athenians also bragged about helping others

---

[23] Ziolkowski 1981 examines the typical structure of a funeral oration and compares the surviving speeches. He provides a useful table of the structure of the orations (on which my table is based) and two tables summarizing the specific items in the *epainos* of each oration (57, 95–97).

[24] Some of these commonplaces are collected and discussed in the glossary of this volume.

[25] See note 15 (p. 13) on Thucydides.

[26] See glossary under **born of the earth**.

[27] See note 25 (p. 50) on Plato.

[28] On these catalogues see Thomas 1989, 196–236; compare introduction to Lysias.

[29] See note 15 (p. 29) on Lysias and note 31 (p. 51) on Plato.

[30] See note 28 (p. 33) on Lysias, introduction to Demosthenes and Hyperides.

in need who came to Athens as suppliants.[31] After this selective narrative of Athenian myth and history, the orators might praise the entire political life of the city of Athens.[32] In addition to these stock topics, other parts of the speech also have an almost formulaic quality. The consolation section regularly addresses the parents and the children of the dead,[33] and the same closing formula often occurs.[34]

But despite all these traditional elements, each oration is also distinctive, and these distinctions are best seen by comparing the speeches. Those of Thucydides and Gorgias have a specific political goal: Thucydides wants to glorify the Athenian democracy in the time of Pericles, and Gorgias protests against Greek in-fighting.[35] The orations of Thucydides and Hyperides both avoid the typical narrative of Athenian achievements and instead emphasize the present. Hyperides casts the conflict with Macedon as a latter-day Persian War by providing a narrative of current events instead of a traditional history of the past. Plato's oration responds to Thucydides in some fashion, whether it is to be regarded as a parody or as a sincere and more accurate praise of Athens.[36] Demosthenes, alone of these writers, must come to terms with a terrible defeat. Lysias' speech is perhaps the most unremarkable, but it gives us a good idea of what a typical funeral oration may have looked like.

Indeed, given all the distinctive aspects of these orations, we should perhaps be cautious about assuming there is such a thing as "a typical funeral oration." The state funeral ceremony was observed regularly in Athens for more than one hundred years and we have only these few speeches to study. Scholars often point to the vapid commonplaces in the speeches and characterize the genre as repetitive and predictable. The speech of Thucydides is much admired, but the others, aside from that of Hyperides, which is labeled as an anomaly, are regarded as part of a decaying and fossilized tradition. It is perhaps more sensible to begin with a speech like that of Lysias, which, however typical it may or may not be, is not influenced by the authorial needs of a Thucydides or Plato, who must adapt their speeches to the surrounding context. Thucydides needed to recast the original speech of Pericles to idealize that time and draw out the contrast between Pericles and later leaders in Athens.[37] Plato's speech was influenced by his philosophic be-

---

[31] See note 23 (p. 31) on Lysias.
[32] See glossary under **constitution** and note 19 (p. 14) on Thucydides.
[33] See note 41 (p. 20) on Thucydides.
[34] Thucydides 46, Plato 249c, Demosthenes 37: "depart."
[35] See introductions to Thucydides and Gorgias.
[36] See introduction to Plato.
[37] See introduction to Thucydides.

liefs,[38] and these can best be identified by comparing that speech with another speech, such as Lysias'. One needs to read more than one funeral oration to appreciate how untypical the speeches of Pericles or Hyperides were. Likewise, a passage as singular as Demosthenes' catalogue of Eponymous Heroes could not appear in a predictable speech.[39]

This volume has collected all of the surviving Athenian funeral orations in the hope that readers will compare the various speeches. Readers who study more than one speech will be able to judge how typical any particular speech is, and also to appreciate the variety and innovation found within each of these orations.

II. Reference systems

Particular passages of works of classical literature are usually cited according to a standard reference scheme, so that readers may identify a passage regardless of the edition or translation of the text being using. All of the speeches in this volume are divided into numbered chapters or sections, which are indicated in the outside margin. Standard references to Thucydides are usually found in the form "book, chapter, section", but since the entire funeral oration given here occurs in book 2, references to that speech in this volume omit the book number. Thus "45.2" = "2.45.2" and refers to the section beginning with the sentence "If I must make ...". Although these numbers are in the margin, the new section actually begins at a major sense break, nearly always after a period. In that same example of Thucydides 2.45.2, the phrase "unantagonistic enthusiasm" is part of 2.45.1. References to Lysias, Demosthenes and Hyperides are by section number, and in the same way the section actually begins with a new sentence in the line indicated. The text of Plato is referred to by Stephanus pages, which are each divided into five (three on the first page of a new dialogue) lettered sections. Thus, Plato *Menexenus* 237c contains the beginning of the paragraph that starts "All mankind ...." Because these Plato references originated with the printed pages of a particular edition, there's not usually any special sense break at the beginning of a new section. The fragments of Gorgias are labeled with the fragment numbers of the modern editors Diels and Kranz. To save space, references to the speeches in this volume all leave out the name of the work. Thus "Demosthenes 28" is an abbreviation for "Demosthenes 60.28," referring to section 28 of oration 60, the funeral oration.

III. Further reading

Pritchett 1985, 102–124 is an excellent, although technical, summary of all of the evidence for the burial ceremony, speech and games. Loraux 1986 offers the most extensive analysis of the funeral oration genre.

---

[38] See introduction to Plato.
[39] See introduction to Demosthenes.

Her chapters focus on: the common *topoi* of the surviving speeches; the importance of the orations for their citizen audience; the speeches' presentation of a unified Athens without class differences; the terms which are used to praise democracy; the *epitaphios* as a genre; and finally, the influence of that genre on other Attic authors. Parker 1996, 131–141 considers the importance of the institution in democratic Athens. He summarizes the controversy over the origin of the public burial, and concludes that the custom must have evolved in stages from the time of Solon's prohibition of private funeral monuments. He also discusses the function of the social institution and the ideology of the funeral orations. Burgess 1902, 146–157 is still very useful, particularly for its catalogue of the occurrences of typical themes in the laudatory sections of the speeches. Another volume from Focus Publishing has also considered two of these orations, with a particular interest in political theory (Collins and Stauffer 1999).

Introduction

Thucydides, an Athenian, wrote a history of the Peloponnesian War and the events that led to that conflict. The Athenians and their naval alliance (on the Delian League see note 17 (p. 14) below) fought the Spartans and their Peloponnesian allies. Open hostilities began in 431 and continued with little interruption until the Athenians surrendered in 404. Most of our knowledge about the historian Thucydides comes from his own writing. He served as a general for the Athenians in 424/3 (4.104.4), and after losing the important Athenian colony of Amphipolis to the Spartan general Brasidas, he was sent into exile for twenty years (5.26.5). Thucydides was born not very long before 454 and died around 400.

He began to write his history early in the war, and continued rewriting over the last thirty years of his life. The history breaks off during the events of 411. In addition to providing a narrative of historical events, Thucydides, like other ancient historians, also recreates several long speeches. The author explains in the introduction to his work that the speeches are reconstructed on the basis of probability with an attempt to hold as closely as possible to what was actually said.[1] He claims to have heard many of the actual speeches he later incorporated into his writing, and he talked to witnesses about other speeches (1.22.1). But the various speeches in the history have a certain consistency in style that is probably due to reworking by Thucydides.[2]

Thucydides particularly admired the Athenian statesman Pericles, who was the foremost leader in Athens until his death from the plague in September 429, only two and a half years after the outbreak of the Peloponnesian War (Thucydides 2.65). The historian contrasts Pericles with his successors, especially Cleon, and his presentation of the character Pericles and the funeral oration he gave in 431 is colored by subsequent events.[3] Many of the speeches in Thucydides come in antithetical pairs, with each speech expressing one side of an argument. The

---

[1] Thucydides 1.22.1: "[speeches] are presented in accordance with what I think each speaker would have been likely to say about his respective affairs. I have kept as close as possible to the overall intention of what was really said." This statement, with its contradiction between what was actually said and what Thucydides supposes a speaker would have stated on any given occasion, is notoriously difficult to interpret. Rusten 1989, 7–17 provides a good discussion of the problem.

[2] References to "Pericles" saying this or that in this volume should be understood to mean "Pericles, as depicted by Thucydides".

[3] Thucydides' summary of the career of Pericles (2.65) was written much later and compares Pericles and his successors. In the funeral oration

funeral oration was delivered at a religious festival, not a political debate, and no reply would be expected, but after the speech Thucydides
immediately narrates the outbreak of a catastrophic plague in Athens
(430–427), which killed some 25% of the population. His description of
the lawlessness that results (2.53) could be seen as an counterbalance
to the previous praise of democracy.

Pericles delivered the funeral oration in the winter of 431, at the end
of the first year of the Peloponnesian war. Thucydides reproduces this
speech at the conclusion of his narrative of that year of the war. This
is one of the most famous passages in all of Greek prose, and it is the
most often studied funeral oration, but it is unusual in that the body
consists of a long description of the Athenian way of life, while the typical account of past Athenian glories is omitted entirely.[4] Has Thucydides adjusted the actual speech to highlight his own interest in Athenian democracy and imperialism? Readers may compare the speech of
Lysias, for example, to see how brief and pointed the Periclean oration
is. These traits may be inherent to the original speech, but they must
also be influenced by Thucydides' goal of depicting the eventual down-
fall of Athens.

This translation owes much to the valuable commentary by Jeffrey
Rusten (Rusten 1989).

---

34   That winter the Athenians, in observance of their ancestral custom,
held a public burial for the men who died first in this war, in the follow-
2   ing way.[5] They set up a tent and lay out the bones of the departed for
three days, and anyone who wishes can bring offerings for his relatives.
3   Then the procession occurs, with wagons leading cypress chests, one for
each tribe.[6] Inside are the bones of the tribe, of whichever tribe each
was a member. One empty bier is carried, made up for the lost ones
4   who were not found for recovery. Whoever wishes, both from the citizens and foreigners,[7] joins the procession, and women family members
5   come to the grave to lament. They put the dead in a public grave, which
is in the most splendid neighborhood of the city, and they always bury

---

Thucydides seems to have especially emphasized the positive aspects
of Athenian democracy, no doubt already prominent in the real speech
Pericles delivered, so that he might more clearly demonstrate how the
state became corrupt under the influence of later leaders such as Cleon.

[4] See glossary under **constitution** and note 19 (p. 14) below.

[5] This chapter provides the only detailed description of the institution of
the public burial.

[6] On the Athenian tribes, see note 44 (p. 71) on Demosthenes.

[7] "Foreign" is *xenos* here. A *xenos* is a fellow Greek, connected by reciprocal expectations of hospitality. See also glossary under **barbarian**.

the dead from war there, except for those who died at Marathon.[8] For
in that case, because they judged the virtue of those men to be magnifi-
6 cent, they buried them on the spot.[9] After they cover them with earth,
a man is chosen by the city, who seems to have an especially wise mind
and fitting character, and he delivers suitable praise over them. After
7 this the people depart. The burial is conducted in this way. Throughout
the entire war, whenever the occasion arose, they observed this custom.
8 Over these men who died first Pericles the son of Xanthippus was chosen to speak. When the time came, he came forward from the grave to
the elevated stage, so that he might be heard by as much of the crowd
as possible, and spoke like this.

35 "Most of those who have spoken here before praise the one who
added this speech to the traditional ceremony, in the belief that it is
good for it to be spoken over those who died in war.[10] Since these men
were brave in their deeds,[11] I thought that these honors, which you
now see being publicly celebrated at this grave, should be displayed
with a deed, and that our belief in the virtues of many men should not
2 depend upon one man, who may speak well or poorly.[12] It is difficult
to speak properly when the plausibility of the truth itself is doubted.
The knowledgeable and well-intentioned listener would probably find
that the presentation falls short of what he wants and knows, while
the inexperienced listener,[13] because of his jealousy, would think that
some qualities are being exaggerated, if he should hear of anything that
surpasses his own nature. Praise of others is bearable only as long as
each listener supposes that he is also capable of doing himself whatever
he hears about. But because people become jealous at the excessiveness
3 of these speeches they accordingly also distrust them.[14] But since men
long ago decided that this is a good custom, I too must observe it and
endeavor to meet the desire and expectation of each of you as much as
possible.

36 I will begin with their ancestors first.[15] It is just and fitting at the

---

[8] On the battle of Marathon see note 29 (p. 33) on Lysias.

[9] See glossary under **virtue**.

[10] "Traditional ceremony" is *nomos*, which describes a traditional custom,
or more specifically, a city law. On the term see below note 22 (p. 15).
For other references to earlier speakers see note 10 (p. 28) on Lysias.

[11] See glossary under **brave** and **speech and deeds**.

[12] On this theme see note 6 (p. 64) on Demosthenes.

[13] In contrast, Hyperides (2) makes no concessions to audience members
who didn't know the dead. He implies that the audience knows the
dead and can fill in any missing details about them.

[14] Demosthenes (23) also worries about jealousy arising from his speech.

[15] Ancient rhetorical treatises list the *genos* as the first required topic in
a funeral oration (Menander Rhetor, 420.11) and in other funeral ora-

same time on an occasion like this to give the honor of that memory
to them. The same people have always settled this region and through
a succession of generations up until this time they handed it on to us

2 as a free land because of their virtue.[16] Not only those men, but also
our fathers deserve praise. In addition to what they received, they ex-
panded the empire to its current size and with great effort they passed

3 it on to us who live now.[17] We ourselves, who are now alive and established as adults, further increased most of it, and we made the city

4 self-sufficient in all respects for war and peace. I will pass over their
deeds in war, with which they acquired each possession, and how they
and our fathers eagerly warded off foreign and Greek attackers, since I
do not wish to speak at length among those who already know of these
deeds.[18] What sort of practices have brought us to this point; what
sort of constitution made this city great; what customs?[19] I will reveal
these first, then I will proceed to praise these men. I think that speaking of these matters is especially appropriate at the present occasion,

---

tions we see that celebration of the Athenians' "nobility of birth" (*eu-
geneia*) regularly includes the standard topics of the fruits of Attica
and autochthony (Plato 237b–238b and Demosthenes 4–5). Thucydides
hints at the latter theme with the description of the "self-sufficient"
(*autarchēs*) city below (36.3), which he develops later (38.2). See also
Lysias 17–19 and Hyperides 7.

[16] See glossary under **born of the earth**.

[17] The Delian League, formed in 478/7, was originally a defensive alliance
centered in the Aegean sea and designed to ward off the Persians.
Athens soon assumed the leading role in the league and gradually
transformed it into an empire chiefly serving her own interests. This
domination eventually brought Athens into conflict with Sparta and
its allies. This conflict, known as the Peloponnesian War (431–404), is
the subject of Thucydides' history.

[18] On the rhetorical device of *praeteritio* see note 7 (p. 79) on Hyperides.
This oration is unusual in that it does not include any narrative of the
accomplishments of the dead or their ancestors. Compare the long account of Athenian glories in Lysias 3–66, and also Plato 239a–246b and
Demosthenes 6–11. Like Thucydides, Hyperides also foregoes the typical catalogue of past accomplishments in favor of more recent deeds
(see note 11 (p. 80) on Hyperides).

[19] After praising the *genos* other orations proceed to the topic of education, or *paideia* (see Plato 237c–238b and Hyperides 8), which Thucydides barely touches upon with his reference to the "practices" and
"customs" of the dead. Praise of the constitution, or *politeia*, is not
in and of itself unusual (see Plato 238c–239a and Demosthenes 25–26),
but the length devoted to the topic by Thucydides is. See glossary under **constitution**.

and that this whole crowd of citizens and non-citizens will profit from hearing these things.[20]

37   We enjoy a constitution that does not emulate our neighbors' laws, and we ourselves act more as an example for someone than as imitators of others. In name it is called a democracy because the government is not in the hands of the few but of the many.[21] In private disagreements, everyone enjoys equality according to the laws. But for public office each is chosen according to worth and particular distinctions, not at random but because of virtue. Furthermore if someone is poor, but able to do the city some good, he is not hindered by the obscurity of
2   his reputation. We govern with tolerance in public affairs and in our suspicion of each other's daily practices. We do not become angry at our neighbor if he does as he pleases, nor do we put on our faces looks of
3   annoyance, which are harmless, but painful. Although in private affairs we associate without offense, in public matters we are especially law-abiding because of respect and obedience to whoever is in power and to the laws, especially the ones that were enacted to aid those that have been treated unjustly, and the ones that, although they are unwritten, confer acknowledged shame.[22]

38   Furthermore, we give the mind many breaks from toil, with customary games and sacrifices all year long. There are also elegant private establishments, and our daily delight in them drives away pain.[23]

---

[20] For foreigners in the ceremony and perhaps also the grave see note 60 (p. 41) on Lysias.

[21] Thucydides describes the political power of the popular assembly. Others translate: "... for the few but for the many." For a discussion of the paragraph see Harris 1992 (163–165 on this sentence). In this paragraph Thucydides refers to some of the key values of Athenian democracy: equality and respect for the law. Plato (238c–239a) and Demosthenes (26) also highlight similar qualities in the Athenian government. The frequent contrast between democracy and oligarchy calls to mind Sparta, Athens' enemy in the Peloponnesian War.

[22] Respect for the law was a fundamental aspect of Athenian ideology. The other key passage for this attitude is the Ephebic oath sworn by all the Athenian males when they were enrolled as citizens and commenced mandatory military training at the age of eighteen: "... I will respect whoever is in power with a good attitude, and also the laws that are in place and those which will be put in place in the future ..." (full text and discussion in Harding 1985, no. 109). The rule of the law was viewed as a fundamental aspect of a free society, opposed to they rule of one, or tyranny. This contrast is vividly drawn by Hyperides (25).

[23] The Athenian calendar was full of festivals and their naval power allowed them to import easily goods from abroad. An anonymous critic of the Athenian democracy, known as the "old oligarch," complains specif-

2 Everything from everywhere comes into the city because of its greatness, and we are able to enjoy our native goods and the products of
other people without a local preference.

39   Our training for war differs from the opposition in these respects:
we make the city open and at no time do we expel anyone, or restrict
them from learning or seeing something which, if it were uncovered and
seen by the enemy, might be useful.[24] We do not trust provisions and
deceit more than our inborn courage for work. In their schooling others pursue manly courage with laborious exercises beginning at a young
age.[25] But although we live in a relaxed manner, we are no less inclined
2 to go into equivalent dangers. Here's proof: the Lacedaemonians do not
campaign against our land by themselves, but with all their allies, while
we, when we invade our neighbors' land, by ourselves easily win most
of the time, even when fighting in a foreign land against men who are
3 defending their own property.[26] No enemy has encountered our collective power because we simultaneously pay attention to the navy and
send our citizens to many places by land. If they encounter and defeat
a portion of our men, they boast that they drove all of us off. If they
4 were defeated, that they were defeated by all of us. And since we are
willing to take risks with a relaxed attitude, not because of laborious
training, and we have courage based in our character more than laws,
we are able not to worry at anticipated troubles, and when we enter
into them we are able to appear no less daring than men who are always working. This city deserves to be admired both in these situations
and also in others.

40   We love nobility without extravagance and wisdom without soft-
ness. We treat wealth as an opportunity for action, not boasting, and
it is not shameful for someone to admit being poor, but it is shameful

---

ically about the excessive number of festivals celebrated in Athens and
also about the importation of luxurious foreign goods (Xenophon, *Constitution of the Athenians*, 3.2 and 2.7; other parallels are collected by
Rusten 1989, 148).

24 Throughout this paragraph Thucydides refers to the Spartans, who
were famous for their secrecy in regard to civic affairs and for their
old-fashioned education system, which gave special attention to
military training. For a general description of the Spartan political
state, written by an admiring Athenian, see Xenophon's *Constitution
of the Spartans*.

25 See glossary under **manly courage**; the same term (*andreia*) is re-
peated in 39.4 below.

26 Lysias repeatedly refers to a few Athenians beating numerous opponents (see note 31 (p. 33) on Lysias). Hyperides also praises the dead
for being victorious even in enemy territory (38). These claims are usually exaggerated for the occasion.

2 not to avoid poverty with action.[27] The same men attend to political affairs and their own households simultaneously, and others, although they pursue their own business, are well aware of political matters.[28] We alone believe that someone who does not have a role in these affairs is not just unpolitical, but useless. We judge political policy correctly even if we did not originate it, because we do not believe that speech is harmful to action, but failure to consider a matter in speech before 3 it must be approached in act is harmful. We are unusual in that the same people are not only daring, but also rational in our endeavors. In others ignorance confers courage and rational thought brings delay. Those who most clearly comprehend their fears and delights and who do not turn away from danger because of them should justly be consid- 4 ered the strongest in their souls.[29] And in virtue we differ from most people. We acquire friends not by receiving favors, but by doing them. Someone who does a favor is more reliable and his good intentions to- ward the one he helped preserve the debt of gratitude. But the one who owes the favor is more sluggish because he knows that he will re- 5 pay virtue not as a favor but as a debt. We alone fearlessly help others, with no calculation of profit, but with trust in freedom.[30]

41   In summary, I say that our whole city is an education for Greece and that each one of us by himself seems to me to be physically self- 2 sufficient in all sorts of situations and very flexible in his favors.[31] The very power of the city, which we have come to possess because of these characteristics, reveals that these are not just boastful words for the 3 present occasion, but true achievements. This is the only city today that turns out to be greater than reported. In the case of this city alone, an attacking enemy does not resent the harm he suffers at the hands

---

27 "Action" (*erga*) is contrasted with speaking ("boasting" and "admit"). Thucydides is particularly fond of this contrast. See glossary under **speech and deeds**.

28 Athens was a direct democracy, in which each citizen was encouraged to take part in the government directly, not through a representative. Able-bodied citizens were also expected to contribute to the war ef- fort, as Thucydides emphasizes below by saying that the same people planned and fought the wars (40.2).

29 Demosthenes (17) also describes rational thought as the precursor to bravery on the battlefield, in a variation of the common contrast be- tween words and deeds (see glossary under **speech and deeds**). Gor- gias (6) makes a similar link between the mental deliberation and phys- ical accomplishments of the fallen.

30 On Athenian aid for suppliants see note 23 (p. 31) on Lysias.

31 Although he doesn't use the term, Thucydides may be alluding to the moderate, or *epieikēs*, nature of the Athenians in regard to suppliants. See glossary under **fairness**.

of such men. No subjects complain that they are not ruled by wor-
4 thy men. Because of these great demonstrations of the power we wield,
which has not gone unnoticed, we will be admired by men now and men
later. We have no additional need for Homer as a praiser nor anyone
else who produces temporary delight with his verses although the truth
of action will work against his intention.[32] We have made all of the sea
and the earth accessible for our daring and we have established eter-
5 nal memorials to our harmful and good deeds.[33] Because these men
thought they should not be deprived of such a city, they fought nobly
and died, and all of us who survive should be willing to work for it.

42   I have spoken at length about the city so that I may show you that
we do not compete on an equal footing with those who have none of
these qualities, and so that I may prove my eulogy for these men over
2 whom I am now speaking. And the most important parts of it have
already been said. For the virtues of these men, and men like them,
created that beauty I was praising in the city. This speech would not appear to match the deeds of any other Greeks but these. I think that this
end now for these men has revealed each man's virtue, either as a first
3 indication or as a final confirmation. Some of them may have been im-
perfect in other matters, but we should rightly give preference to their
courage against their enemies on behalf of their fatherland. By elimi-
nating evil for the common good they did more help than the sum of
4 their individual injuries.[34] As for these men, not one of the wealthy ones
turned coward because he preferred to continue enjoying his wealth, nor
did any poor man avoid the terror in the hope that he might become
wealthy if he should escape.[35] They preferred to punish their enemies
and they believed that this was a very noble danger to face, and so they
decided to punish those men despite these risks and they volunteered
to give up everything else. They entrusted the uncertainty of the future to hope, but they trusted their own achievements with regard to
what they could already see. Because they thought that fighting and

---

[32] The Greek heroes of the Persian Wars were celebrated soon afterward in
works by poets such as Simonides, who wrote elegiac poems on the battles of Artemisium and Plataea (the fragments are translated in West
1993, 168–172). Elsewhere, in an important chapter on method, Thucydides describes his entire work as a "possession for always" in contrast
to these sorts of "temporary delights" (1.22.4). Other speakers also refer to earlier poetic or musical dedications to the dead (Plato 239c and
Lysias 3).

[33] Greek morality encouraged one to harm his enemies. Some editors
emend to "noble and good deeds."

[34] See glossary under **public and private**.

[35] Plato (246d–e) echoes this passage with the emphasis on shame and the
assertion that there can be no goods in a life tainted by cowardice.

suffering were more appropriate than surrendering and surviving, they avoided any shameful talk with their act of physical resistance. And through the chance of the briefest moment, at the height of glory, not fear, they departed.[36]

43   The character of these men matched their city. We who remain must pray to have a safer spirit toward the enemy, but we must also value one that is no less daring. We must consider their contribution not just with this one speech, which could be extended with a description of all their good achievements in the defense against the enemies, material you yourselves know just as well as the speaker. Instead we must look to the real day-to-day power of the city and we must become its lovers,[37] and, as we consider its greatness, we must keep in mind that all this was acquired by men who were daring, who knew what needed to be done, and who were honorable in their achievements. If they failed in an attempt for something, they did not because of that decide to deprive the city of their own virtue, but instead they gave their noblest

2   contribution to it. Because they gave their lives for the common good, they received ageless praise individually and a tomb most distinctive.[38] They don't rest there; instead their glory eternally awaits any occasion

3   for speech or action that may arise.[39] The whole earth is a tomb for distinguished men. At home the inscription on the grave-stones identifies the grave, but not only that, elsewhere an unwritten memorial also re-

4   mains for each one in people's minds, not on stone. If you admire these men and consider happiness to be freedom and freedom to be bravery,

5   you must not disregard the dangers of war. It is no more right for those who are bad off, who don't have any hope of success, to give up their

---

[36] Rusten 1986 analyzes this passage in great detail. He points out the compact description of the sequence of events that leads to the soldiers' willingness to sacrifice themselves: first they decide to enter battle in pursuit of glory, then they put aside thought of their own future and devote themselves to the matter at hand, finally they achieve glory by consenting to die. See also glossary under **danger**. Demosthenes (26) describes this same sequence of events, beginning with the soldiers' fear of shame and ending with their noble death.

[37] Monoson 2000, 64–87 discusses this striking metaphor in great detail, in which she sees an emphasis on the reciprocal nature of the relationship between citizens and the city. She focuses on the term *erastēs*, or "lover", which is regularly used of the active partner in a sexual relationship, and argues that this term emphasizes a voluntary, rather than obligatory, role in politics. She also connects this masculine expression with the attitude toward women expressed by Pericles in 45.2

[38] "Ageless praise" is a common motif in later funeral orations: compare Lysias 79–81, Demosthenes 32 and Hyperides 42.

[39] See glossary under **speech and deeds**.

lives, than those who risk a reversal in life and who stand to lose the
6 most, if they falter at all.[40] The degradation that comes with cowardice
is more grievous for a brave man than death, which is painless because
of his strength and shared hope.

44   For these reasons I do not pity all of you parents who are here, but
I will offer consolation.[41] They know that they raised their children
in varied circumstances. But it is fortunate to receive what is most
glorious, death for these men, and grief for you. Their happiness was
2 allotted throughout life and included death. I know that it is difficult
to persuade you, since you will often see the good fortunes of others, in
which you yourselves also used to take pleasure, as reminders of them.
Grief does not occur when someone is deprived of some unused good,
3 but rather at the loss of something depended upon. They should find
strength in the hope for other children, if they are still the right age
to have them. New children will help some individuals to forget the
dead, and they will replace a loss in the city and keep it safe. Those
who do not expose their own children to risk on an equal basis cannot
4 offer counsel that is at all fair or just. As for those of you who are
too old to have more children, count the majority of your life, as long
as you were fortunate, as a profit. The remainder will be brief, and it
will be softened by their glory. Love of honor is the only ageless thing,
and in useless old age profit is not as pleasing, whatever others may
45 say, as honor. I see a great struggle for all you children and for the
brothers of these men. Everyone is accustomed to praise the dead, and
you will not be judged equal, on account of their supreme virtue, but
slightly inferior. A living competitor is envied, but after he is gone he is
2 honored with unantagonistic enthusiasm. If I must make some mention
of womanly virtue, for those of you who will be widows, I will say it all
with a little advice.[42] The greatest glory comes from not being inferior
to your nature and having the least reputation for virtue or reproach
among men.

---

[40] The speaker considers cowardice a worse evil than death, as he explains
in the next sentence.

[41] Whereas Pericles' praise of the dead, with it's abstract depiction of
Athenian democracy, departed from more traditional narratives of past
Athenian glories, this speech's formal consolation, or *paramythia*, is
more typical. After addressing the assembly in general in the previous paragraph, he now singles out the parents of the dead, then their
children, and finally their wives. Similarly, Plato (246d–249c) addresses
a long section to the parents and children of the dead. See also Lysias
77–80, Demosthenes 32–37 and Hyperides 41–43.

[42] Scholars have tried to interpret this injunction to the widows in a positive light, but Rusten 1989, 175–176 argues against such efforts. The
other orations provide no parallels.

46   In accordance with the law, I have addressed the appropriate points in my speech. With their acts, these men now being buried have already adorned themselves. But their children will be raised from now on at public expense until they reach adolescence, a useful prize to these men and their survivors for their great struggles.[43] Those who offer the greatest prizes for virtue also have the best citizens governing. But now that you have lamented these men as each of you should, depart."

---

[43] On the state support of the orphans see note 72 (p. 61) on Plato.

Introduction

Gorgias was active at roughly the same time as Thucydides. He was born around 480 and lived until after 380. During the Peloponnesian War, in 427, he came to Athens from his native Leontini in Sicily. He quickly became known for his style of oratory and writing, which featured stiffly balanced clauses, antithesis, and rhymes. Critics could charge Gorgias with being more concerned with the way his compositions sounded than with what they meant, but his style was widely influential at Athens and elsewhere. Gorgias became a teacher of rhetoric, one of the so-called "sophists." These highly-paid teachers emphasized cleverness in speech, and their students hoped to profit from their expensive education by being persuasive speakers in the courts and assembly in Athens. In his play the *Clouds*, the comic poet Aristophanes stereotypes Socrates as such a teacher, and the end of the play presents an animated contest between the old style of education and the new style of teaching of the Sophists. Gorgias himself also appears as a character in Plato's dialogue, the *Gorgias*, where he asserts the importance of learning rhetoric for its own sake.

Little of Gorgias' writing survives. The only complete works are both speeches on mythical subjects. One praises Helen, often blamed for causing the Trojan War, and the other defends Palamedes, who was charged with betraying the Greeks during the Trojan War.[1] Gorgias' funeral oration survives only in fragments, and some of these are quoted for their ridiculousness (5a) and may not be representative of the entire speech. The oration criticized the Athenians' fighting against fellow-Greeks (5b), and was probably composed during the Peloponnesian War. This criticism stands apart from Pericles' praise of the Athenian system and their superiority over other Greeks. It is very unlikely that Gorgias actually delivered this oration, though, since he was not a citizen in Athens. The speech was probably written as a demonstration speech for his students, as an example of what a funeral oration should look like. In the introduction of Plato's *Menexenus*, Socrates tells of hearing such a demonstration speech from Aspasia (236b), and Gorgias may have similarly delivered this speech for his students.

---

[1] On the former see MacDowell 1982, which features an excellent introduction and an English translation in addition to a Greek text with notes; on the latter see Usher 1999, 360–363.

Fragment 1

5a Xerxes, the Zeus of the Persians[2]

Fragment 2

Vultures are living tombs.

Fragment 3

5b Trophies over the barbarians call for hymns of praise, those over Greeks call for lamentations.[3]

Fragment 4

6 What was lacking in these men that should be present in men?[4] What was present which should not be present? I hope to be able to say what I desire, and I hope to desire what is needed, avoiding divine retribution and escaping mortal jealousy. For these men possessed virtue that was full of the divine, and mortality that was human.[5] Many times they preferred gentle fairness to bold justice,[6] and many times the correctness of words to strict law, because they believed this to be the most divine and universal law: to say and not say and do and not do the right thing at the right time.[7] They exercised twice as much as they needed to, with their mind and their strength, deliberating with the one and accomplishing with the other.[8] They took care of those who were unjustly unfortunate,[9] and they punished those who were fortunate un-

---

[2] The speech contained an account of the Persian War, which was often included in the catalogue of Athenian history in such speeches. Lysias 20–47 is the longest account, and the only other surviving one that names Xerxes (27). Xerxes was the Persian king who led the second campaign against the Greeks, in 480, ten years after his father Darius' first expedition was defeated at Marathon.

[3] Philostratus, an Athenian writer active in the third century AD, states that Gorgias had a political agenda in his funeral oration (*Lives of the Sophists* 1.9 (493)). He advocated a reconciliation between the Greek states involved in the Peloponnesian War. This policy was openly espoused in his *Olympic Oration*, and in his funeral oration he made his point by concentrating on the victories over the Persians and not mentioning any discord among the Greeks. See glossary under **barbarian**.

[4] This passage must have come from the main section of the speech praising the fallen.

[5] See glossary under **virtue**.

[6] See glossary under **fairness**.

[7] "And not do" has been added into the text by a modern editor.

[8] On this expression see note 29 (p. 17) on Thucydides.

[9] On this euphemism, see note 39 (p. 35) on Lysias.

justly.[10] They were strongly willed toward anything beneficial and they favored propriety. With their sensible minds they checked their insensible strength. They were outrageous toward the outrageous, well behaved toward the well behaved, fearless toward the fearless, fearful toward the fearful.[11] As witnesses to these facts they raised trophies over the enemy, statues for Zeus, dedications for themselves. They were not inexperienced in the inborn spirit for war, or in traditional desires, or in strife in arms, or in honorable peace. They were respectful toward the gods with their justice, pious toward their parents with their care, just toward the citizens with their equality, dutiful toward friends with their trust. Now that they have died our longing for them does not die with them, but it lives on for those who do not live, immortal in bodies that are not immortal.

---

[10] Hyperides (5) similarly juxtaposes Athenian aid for those in need and their punishment of the unjust. See note 5 (p. 79) on Hyperides.

[11] "Outrageous" is *hybristēs*, an adjective that describes somebody who commits hubris (note 48 (p. 72) on Demosthenes). The opposite is "well behaved" (kosmios). This sort of word-play, with parallel antithetical clauses and repetition of keywords, was typical of Gorgias' style, and many Attic authors were influenced by him. See note 68 (p. 59) on Plato.

Introduction

Lysias was born in Athens, probably in the 440s, the son of Cephalus, a foreign resident in Athens, from Syracuse in Sicily. As the child of a foreigner, he did not have citizenship in Athens, and lived there as a *metic*, or resident alien, like his father. Lysias emigrated to the colony of Thurii in Sicily, probably around 430. At this time Sicily had a reputation as a center of rhetorical training.[1] Lysias returned to Athens in 412 amid a climate of anti-Athenian feelings in the wake of the unsuccessful campaign of the Athenians against the Syracusans and their allies (415–413). His family operated a successful business producing shields in the Piraeus, the port city of Athens. At the end of the Peloponnesian War the ruling faction in Athens appropriated much of the family's property and executed Lysias' brother Polemarchus.[2] Lysias escaped and supported the democratic faction and after their successful return to Athens he was granted citizenship in 403 only to have it revoked on a technicality. Lysias delivered a speech (Lysias, oration 12) prosecuting one of the tyrants who had killed his brothers. This case must have brought attention to Lysias, since he was later able to earn his living by running a school of oratory and by writing persuasive speeches for clients to use in the courtroom. Many of these speeches, dating from 403 to around 380, survive and Lysias is admired as a stylist who could adopt various individualized tones to suit each of his clients' cases.

Since Lysias was not a citizen in Athens, he almost certainly did not deliver his funeral oration himself. Speechwriting was not well regarded in Athens, on the grounds that it gave an unfair advantage to litigants who were wealthy enough to commission speeches. It is unlikely that any prominent citizen who was given the honor of delivering the funeral oration would have used a speech written by a professional speechwriter. This funeral oration should be regarded as a similar product to the speech of Gorgias, designed as a model for use in a school setting.

Lysias' funeral oration was composed during the Corinthian War,[3] probably in the late 390s. This speech appears to be an example of a typical funeral oration of the period. Unlike Thucydides, it does not highlight the current-day political system of Athens,[4] but instead

---

[1] Plato (*Phaedrus* 267a) presents a catalogue of Sophists from various regions, including Gorgias and Tisias from Sicily.

[2] On this period, see note 55 (p. 40) below.

[3] See note 61 (p. 41) below.

[4] See glossary under **constitution**.

presents a long historical narrative of Athenian history.[5] The narrative is selective and often inaccurate, intended to distinguish the Athenians from the other Greeks. The Athenians defended Greece from foreign adversaries, most notably during the Persian Wars, and protected foreign suppliants.[6] One may also compare Lysias' brief treatment of the Athenians' wars against other Greeks (61–65) with the longer narrative in Plato (242e–244b). Compared to Lysias, Plato displays an unusual interest in the Peloponnesian War and the Athenian civil war, topics which are usually avoided in these catalogues of Athenian history.

———

1 You who are present at this grave: if I thought it possible to present in a speech the virtue of the men lying here,[7] I would have found fault with those who called upon me a few days ago to speak over them. But since all eternity is not sufficient for any person to match in a speech the deeds of these men,[8] because of this I think that the city also, out of forethought for those who speak here, makes the appointment on short notice, because it believes that in this way the speakers will receive
2 extra sympathy from their listeners.[9] Although I am speaking about these men, I do not compete with their deeds, but rather with those who have spoken over the dead previously.[10] The virtue of these men has provided such an abundance of material, both for those who are capable of acting and for those who want to speak, that, although many things have been well said by those who spoke about them before, much has also been left out by those orators, and there remains enough their successors to say. There was not any land or sea which these men didn't know, and everywhere and among all people those who lament their misfortunes also celebrate the virtuous achievements of these men.
3   To begin with, I will go through the ancient exploits of their an-

———

[5] See note 12 (p. 29) below.

[6] See note 28 (p. 33) and note 23 (p. 31) below.

[7] See glossary under **virtue**.

[8] Literally "for all persons." The orator here uses polyptoton of the word "all" (*pas*) for emphasis. See note 68 (p. 59) on Plato on this device. See note 6 (p. 64) on Demosthenes for this general theme.

[9] Menexenus (235c) also refers to the short notice given to speakers, but Socrates responds that such orations are easy to improvise, and in any case speakers would already have prepared speeches suitable for the occasion.

[10] It was customary to refer to earlier orators who had delivered the funeral oration (Thucydides 35.1, Demosthenes 1). See also glossary under **speech and deeds** on the theme.

cestors,[11] taking my cue from legend.[12] We all should remember those men too, by celebrating them in songs,[13] by making speeches at memorials for brave men,[14] by honoring them at these sorts of occasions, and by teaching the living the deeds of the dead.

4   Long ago, the Amazons were the daughters of Ares, living by the Thermodon river, and they were the only ones armed with iron of all those around them, and the first of all to mount horses, with which, to the surprise of their inexperienced enemies, they captured those who fled from them and left behind those who pursued them.[15] They were considered men because of their courage more than women because of their nature. They seemed to excel over men in their spirits beyond

5   what they lacked in physical form. They were the rulers of many tribes, and they had enslaved those near them by action; when they heard tell of the great glory of this land, because of their own enormous reputation and great ambition, they gathered together the most warlike of the tribes and campaigned against this city.[16] But when they encountered brave men their spirits were like their nature,[17] and, in achieving a reputation that was the opposite of their previous one, they appeared as women more in their reaction to the dangerous events than in their

6   bodies. They alone were not allowed to make better plans after learning from their mistakes. Nor could they return home and publicize their misfortune and the virtue of our ancestors. But by dying here and pay-

---

[11] "Exploits" is the plural of *kindynos*, literally "dangers." Lysias uses the term frequently to describe the risks the Athenians faced. See glossary under **danger**. The word must sometimes be rendered more loosely as here, or 26 ("venture") and 47 ("encounters").

[12] This paragraph begins the longest narrative of earlier Athenian accomplishments, which occupies most of the speech (3–66; compare Plato 239a–246b and Demosthenes 6–11). Other orations may omit this section entirely (see note 18 (p. 14) on Thucydides).

[13] See note 32 (p. 18) on Thucydides for poetic praise of the dead.

[14] The Greek term for "brave" here is literally "good" (*agathos*). See glossary under **brave**.

[15] The Amazons appear frequently in Greek art and literature. They were a mythical race of women renowned for their skill at war who lived on the edge of the world, in Asia minor where the Thermodon river drains into the Black Sea. According to Athenian legend their early king Theseus led the Athenians to ward off an Amazon invasion. They appear in other orations too (Plato 239b and Demosthenes 8). Tyrrell 1984, 13–19 discusses conceptions of the Amazons in the funeral orations and elsewhere.

[16] On "action" (*ergon*) and "hear tell" (*logos*) see glossary under **speech and deeds**.

[17] On the phrase "brave men" (*andres agathoi*) see glossary under **brave**.

ing the penalty for their ignorance, they made the memory of this city immortal on account of its virtue, while they made their own fatherland nameless on account of their misfortune here. Because of their unjust desire for another land, those women justly lost their own.

7   After Adrastus and Polynices campaigned against Thebes and were defeated, the Cadmeans would not allow them to bury their dead.[18] The Athenians believed that those men, if they were at all wrong, by dying had received the greatest punishment, and that the gods below were not receiving what was theirs, and that the gods above were being dishonored when the holy rites were being polluted. At first the Athenian sent heralds, asking the Cadmeans to permit the retrieval of corpses.

8   The Athenians believed that it was a characteristic of brave men to punish their enemies while they were alive, and that demonstrating bravery among the corpses of the dead was typical of men without confidence.[19] When they failed in this request the Athenians campaigned against the Cadmeans, even though there was no previous hostility between them and they didn't owe the current generation of Argives any-

9   thing. Nevertheless, they supposed that the war dead deserved their customary rites, and they risked danger against others for the sake of both sides: for the one side, so that they would no longer commit outrages against the gods by defiling the dead, and for the others, so that they might not go home without receiving the traditional honor, de-

10 prived of a Greek custom and cheated of a universal expectation.[20] The Athenians recognized these things, but they also believed that uncertainty in war is universal for all people.[21] Although they had many enemies, with justice as an ally they prevailed in the fight. They were not inspired by their good luck to exact further punishment on the Cad-

---

18 Polynices was one of the children of Oedipus who campaigned against his brother Eteocles at Thebes with the help of his father-in-law Adrastus. This campaign is the subject of Aeschylus' *Seven against Thebes*. After their death the Thebans, or Cadmeans, did not allow the corpses to be retrieved and buried. Euripides' *Suppliants* tells the story of their mothers' appeal to the mythical king of Athens, Theseus, for help in securing the burial of their sons, and the subsequent Athenian campaign against Thebes. This legend, which not only highlights Athens' aid to suppliants, but also emphasizes the importance of burial for fallen soldiers, is also referred to in other funeral orations (Plato 239b and Demosthenes 8). Parker 1983, 44–48 provides a good summary of Greek attitudes toward the burial of the dead.

19 "Brave men" is *andres agathoi*. See glossary under **brave**.

20 The "universal expectation" (*koinos elpis*) refers to a proper burial for the dead.

21 "Uncertainty" is *tychē*. The same word is translated as "good luck" a few lines below. See glossary under **chance**.

means. Instead, they demonstrated to them their own virtue in place of impiety. They themselves took the prizes for which they had come, the Argive corpses, and buried them in their own Eleusis.[22] With regard to the dead of the Seven against Thebes, this is the sort of men our ancestors were.

11   Later on, after Heracles passed away, his children were fleeing from Eurystheus. They were turned away by all the Greeks, who were ashamed of their own acts, but feared the power of Eurystheus.[23] Then they came to this city and sat down at the altars as suppliants.

12   When Eurystheus demanded their surrender, the Athenians refused to give them up. They respected the virtue of Heracles more than they feared danger to themselves. They also preferred to fight justly in support of the weak, not to indulge the powerful and hand over those who were being wronged by them.

13   When Eurystheus went to war with those who at that time held the Peloponnese as his allies, the Athenians did not change their minds as the danger grew near. Instead they kept the same opinion as before, even though they had not been singled out for any personal favor by the father of these men, and they did not know what sort of men the children would become.

14   But because they thought it was just, although they had no previous enmity toward Eurystheus, and there was no profit to be made except for noble glory, they exposed themselves to such great dangers on the children's behalf. Since they pitied the ones who were being wronged and hated the men committing the violence, they attempted to prevent the latter and were willing to aid the former. They believed that it was a demonstration of freedom to do nothing against their will, and of justice to aid those who were being wronged, and of courage to

15   die fighting for both of these, if they must. They both were so high spirited that Eurystheus and his men were unwilling to find anything

---

22 The term "prizes" (*athla*) regularly refers to the prizes granted to winners of athletic contests. Eleusis, about 15 km northwest of Athens in Attica, was the site of a sanctuary and religious festivals for Demeter and Persephone.

23 The Athenians prided themselves on the aid they gave to suppliants, such as the children of Heracles (the Heraclidae). Other well known examples of this motif from fifth-century tragedy are the protection they afforded to the elderly Oedipus in Sophocles' *Oedipus at Colonus*, or to Orestes in the *Oresteia*, and their efforts to secure burial for the Seven against Thebes, also the subject of a play by Aeschylus (see note 18 (p. 30)). According to myth, Eurystheus, who had forced Heracles to undergo his labors, continued to persecute his children after his death. They sought and received help from Athens. Euripides' *Heraclidae* depicts them as suppliants in Athens. For the Heraclidae elsewhere in funeral orations see also Plato 239b and Demosthenes 8.

in what the Athenians offered willfully, while the Athenians for their part did not approve of Eurystheus, himself a suppliant, taking away their suppliants. They organized a local army and defeated in battle the troops assembled from the whole of the Peloponnese.[24] They secured the safety of the children of Heracles and at the same time by releasing them from fear they also freed their souls. Because of the virtue of their father the Athenians honored those children by

16 themselves taking chances. The children were much more fortunate than their father. He was the cause of much good for all people, but he had made a life of toil and contention and ambition for himself. He chastened other unjust men, but he was not able to punish Eurystheus, who was an enemy of his and had done him wrong. But his children, because of this city, on that same day saw both their own salvation and the punishment of their enemies.

17 Many times our ancestors stood up in solidarity for justice.[25] That's because the beginning of their life was just. For it's not the case, as it is for most, that they were gathered together from everywhere else, and then after expelling others they settled their land. But rather, being born of the earth they possess the same land as both

18 a mother and a fatherland.[26] They were the first, and the only ones at that time, to expel the rulers among them and they established a democracy because they believed that freedom for all provides the greatest unity. Because they shared common hopes arising from the dangers they faced together, they ran their government with free souls.

19 With the law they honored the good and punished the wicked. They thought controlling each other with violence was the mark of beasts. Humans should define justice by law, and be persuasive in speech, and serve both of these goals in their acts, by serving the laws and learning from speech.[27]

20 Because of their noble birth and judgment, the ancestors of the men lying here achieved many fine and amazing deeds. Those who were born from them have also left behind great and memorable trophies everywhere because of their virtue. They alone put themselves at risk for the sake of all of Greece against many tens of thousands of barbarians.[28]

---

24 The word "local" is *idios*, here contrasted with the greater forces of the Peloponnese. The same term often refers to the individual contributions of the fallen dead; see glossary under **public and private**.

25 For praise of the *genos* see note 15 (p. 13) on Thucydides.

26 See glossary under **born of the earth**.

27 "Acts" is *erga*. See glossary under **speech and deeds**. On Athenian respect for the law, see note 22 (p. 15) on Thucydides.

28 See glossary under **barbarian**. Herodotus' *Histories* tell the story of the combined Greek states' defense against the Persian invasions in 490 and 480–479, and also narrate the development of the Persian empire

21 At that time the king of Asia, unsatisfied with the good things he had, also hoped to enslave Europe and sent an army of 500,000. They realized that they would easily rule the other Greeks, if they could either make this city a consenting ally or overwhelm it against its will. They disembarked at Marathon,[29] in the belief that the enemy would have the least allied support if they took a chance while Greece was still in

22 disagreement as to how to defend against the aggressors. Furthermore, they thought highly of our city because of its earlier deeds. They knew that, if they attacked another city first, they would have to fight those people and the Athenians together, because the Athenians would come eagerly to help those in need. But if they landed near Athens first, they suspected that no other Greeks states would dare to declare war openly by saving the Athenians and acting against the Persians to help others.

23 That's what the Persians were thinking. But our ancestors didn't give a thought to the dangers of war. No, they did not fear the great number of enemies; they trusted more in their own virtue in the belief that a glorious death leaves behind an undying account among good men.[30] Our ancestors were ashamed that the foreigners were on their soil and they did not wait for the allies to hear the news and come help. They didn't want to thank others for their safety, but rather they thought the

24 other Greeks should thank them. All of them went to fight in solidarity, few against many.[31] They considered death to be the fate of many, but bravery the fate of few.[32] They also thought that their souls were not re-

---

and many other earlier events of more or less relevance. The Athenian accounts eventually came to celebrate the victories at Marathon (note 29 (p. 33) below) and Salamis (note 40 (p. 36) below) especially, where the Athenians had the largest role. The Persian Wars were the most important event of recent historical times that appears in the typical catalogue of Athenian accomplishments. For discussion of the "Athenian history of Athens" see Loraux 1986, 132–171 and Thomas 1989, 196–236.

[29] In 490 the Athenians, with only the help of the Plataeans, who are forgotten in these speeches, defeated the Persian invaders who had landed at Marathon in Attica. For a narrative of the battle see Herodotus 6.107–113. Athenian public art celebrated this victory alongside the much earlier legend of Theseus' expedition against the Amazons (Pausanias 1.15 on the Stoa Poecile of c. 475 – 450). Compare the account at Plato 240c–e.

[30] "Account" is *logos*, the same word used above (end of 19, translated "speech") to describe the material that instructs the next generation. On the phrase "good men," see glossary under **brave**.

[31] This assertion that a few Athenians could defeat many opponents reoccurs as a motif later in this speech (37, 56; see also Thucydides 39.2).

[32] See glossary under **brave**. The phrase *andres agathoi* occurs again a

ally their own possessions, owing to death, but they could leave behind
their own personal memorial by facing danger. They supposed that if
they could not achieve victory on their own, they still wouldn't be able
to with their allies. If defeated, they reasoned, they would die a little
sooner than the others, but if victorious, they would free the others too.

25 By being brave and generous with their lives, and by not choosing life
over virtue, and by feeling more shame before their own laws than fear
of the danger against the enemy, they established a trophy for Greece
over the barbarians, who had reached beyond the boundaries of their

26 own country to attack another just for money. They made their venture
so quickly that the same men announced to the others the arrival here
of the barbarians and also the victory of our ancestors.[33] None of the
others were even afraid of the coming danger, but they were overjoyed
to hear of their own freedom. As a result it is not surprising, considering all those deeds done long ago, that all mankind even now still envies
their virtue, as if these events had happened recently.

27 Next, after making preparations for ten years, Xerxes, the king of
Asia, arrived with 1200 ships.[34] He despised Greece and his hope had
been thwarted. He was dishonored by what had happened, pained by
the misfortune and angry at those responsible. But he had not himself
suffered the evils and had not personally experienced the brave men.
Now he led a multitude of soldiers on foot, so many that it would be

28 a big task to count up even the tribes that followed him. This is the
best proof of their multitude: although he had 1000 ships to transport
his army across the narrows of the Hellespont from Asia to Europe, he
refused to use them, because he thought it would be a great waste of

29 time. Instead, disdaining the natural order and the divine sphere and
human conceptions, he made a road through the sea. He also forced the
ships to sail through the land, by bridging the Hellespont and cutting
a channel through Athos.[35] Nobody resisted; those who were unwilling
obeyed and those who were willing became traitors. The former were
unable to defend themselves and the latter were corrupted by greed.

30 Two things motivated them: profit and fear. While Greece was occupied with this invasion, the Athenians boarded their ships and came to
the rescue at Artemisium. The Lacedaemonians and some of the allies met the Persians at Thermopylae, thinking they would be able to
prevent the Persian entry there because of the narrowness of the re-

---

little below at the beginning of 25.

[33] Herodotus 6.115–116 describes the Athenians' rushed return to the city
after the battle to protect it from the Persian fleet.

[34] Lysias now refers to the second Persian invasion, ten years after
Marathon, in 480–479.

[35] Herodotus (7.22–24 and 33–37) describes these projects in more detail.
He ascribes them to Xerxes' arrogance.

31 gion.[36] The battles occurred simultaneously: the Athenians were victorious at sea; but the Lacedaemonians were destroyed. Although they were not lacking in bravery,[37] the Lacedaemonians were wrong in their estimates of the number of guards and the number of attackers. They were not defeated by the enemy, because they died where they were

32 stationed to fight.[38] In this way then one side was unlucky,[39] but the other won entry into Greece and was marching toward this city. After they heard of the Lacedaemonians' misfortune, our ancestors did not know how to face the troubles surrounding them. They knew that, if they encountered the barbarians on land, the Persian navy would sail in with 1000 ships and find the city undefended. But if the Athenians boarded their ships, they would be defeated by the army on foot. They didn't have the resources to mount a defense and leave behind

33 a sufficient guard. These were the two choices before them: whether they must abandon their fatherland, or side with the foreigners and enslave the Greeks. They believed that freedom, which comes with virtue, poverty and exile, was better than the enslavement of their fatherland, accompanied by reproach and wealth. They abandoned their city for the sake of Greece, so that they might take their chances on each front

34 in turn and not face both forces at the same time. They transported the children and women to Salamis and assembled the other allies' naval forces.[40] Not many days later both the army and the navy of the bar-

---

36 The battles of Thermopylae and Artemisium occurred simultaneously in the autumn of 480. The Spartans attempted to hold the narrow pass at Thermopylae but were defeated due to the treachery of a local who showed the Persians an alternate route, allowing them to surround the Spartans (Herodotus 7.201–233). The Athenians tend to emphasize the concurrent sea-battle nearby at Artemisium, in which they had a much more prominent role (Herodotus 8.8–23).

37 The word translated here as "bravery" is the plural of *psychē*, or "soul".

38 Demosthenes also asserts that the fallen were not truly defeated because of the nobility of their death (19).

39 Lysias is very fond of this euphemism for defeat and he uses it to refer to various battles. The verb *dystychein* and the related nouns and adjectives are frequent in this speech (see, for example, 39, 58, 68, 70), and also occur in the other orations (Plato 244b, Demosthenes 1).

40 Shortly after the battles of Thermopylae and Artemisium, the Athenian general Themistocles, influenced by an oracle at Delphi, convinced the people to abandon the city of Athens to the Persians. After a protracted battle at sea the Greek forces defeated the Persian navy just off the island of Salamis in the Saronic gulf. See Herodotus 7.141–143 on the oracle and 8.40–97 for the Greek debate over fighting and the narrative of the battle itself. Lysias' emotional account casts this battle as the most significant event of the Persian Wars. The battle was also

barians arrived. Who would not have been frightened to see them? So
great and terrifying was the battle contested by this city to win the
35 freedom of the Greeks![41] What did the witnesses who saw the men on
those ships think, with their own safety and the upcoming contest in
doubt? And what about the men who were about to fight for their loved
36 ones, for those prizes on Salamis? So many enemies surrounded them
on all sides that knowledge of their impending death was the least of
the evils facing them. They were most worried about what they thought
the victorious barbarians would do to the wives and children hidden on
37 Salamis.[42] I suppose that in all the confusion they kept grasping each
other and they probably pitied themselves with good reason, realizing
that their own ships were so few, and seeing that the enemy had many,
and knowing that their city was abandoned, and that the countryside
was being destroyed and was full of foreigners, and that the temples
38 were being burned, and that all terrors were close at hand.[43] At the
same time they heard Greek and foreign battle-songs all mixed together,
and the shouts of both sides and the screaming of the dying. The sea
was full of corpses, and much wreckage from friendly and hostile ships
was sinking everywhere. For a long time the sea battle was an even
match, and at one time they thought they had won and been saved,
39 and then that they had been defeated and destroyed. In their fear I
imagine that they thought they saw many things they didn't, and that
they thought they heard many things they didn't hear. What prayers
to the gods did they not make, or reminders of sacrifices? How much
pity was there for their children and wives, longing and lament for their
fathers and mothers, and reckoning of the evils that would happen if
40 they were unlucky? What god would not have pitied them in the face
of such a great danger? What man would not have wept? Who would
not have marveled at their daring? Those men greatly excelled all hu-
mankind in virtue both with their deliberations and the risks they took
on the battlefield when they left their city, boarded their ships and pit-
ted their lives, although they were few, against the multitude of Asia.
41 They demonstrated to everybody, by winning at sea, that it is better

---

the centerpiece of Aeschylus' *Persians*. Plato's account is much briefer
(241b).

[41] It is difficult to convey the mixed metaphor in the original. The noun
kindynos, literally "danger," is here rendered as "the battle" and just
below as "the contest" (35). The verb relates to *agōn*, the noun used
for various sorts of contests and competitions, such as athletic games.
The latter metaphor continues below in "prizes" (*athla*).

[42] Hyperides (20) develops this worry for the treatment of one's family by
the triumphant enemy.

[43] Herodotus (8.52–54) describes the capture and burning of the temples
on the Acropolis in Athens.

to be on the side of a few men fighting for freedom, not that of many
42 royal subjects fighting for their own slavery. Those men contributed
many fine things for the freedom of the Greeks: the general Themistocles, most capable at judging and acting, more ships than all the other
allies, and the most experienced men. What other other Greeks would
43 have competed with them in judgment, number, and virtue? As a result they received the undisputed award for bravery from Greece at the
sea-battle, and they rightly attained success commensurate with the
dangers they faced. They demonstrated to those barbarians from Asia
that their virtue was genuine and born of the earth.[44]

44   That is how great they were in the sea battle. They undertook
by far the biggest share of the danger, and with their own individual
virtue they made freedom a public commodity for the others Greeks
too.[45] Later on, the Peloponnesians built a wall across the Isthmus.
They were thinking only of their own safety. They supposed that they
were rid of the danger from the sea, and they were content to watch the
45 other Greeks come under the power of the barbarians. But the Athenians in anger advised them that, if they were going to have that attitude,
they'd better build a wall around the whole Peloponnese. If the Athenians themselves were to be betrayed by the Greeks, they said, and if they
were to become subject to the barbarians, then the Persians would not
need a thousand ships and the wall on the Isthmus would not help the
Peloponnesians. Command of the sea would safely belong to the King.
46 The Peloponnesians learned their lesson and they realized that their
plans were unjust and cowardly. The also saw that the Athenians' advice was just and brave, and so they came to help at Plataea.[46] Most of
the allies were afraid of the great multitude of the enemy and abandoned
their posts during the night, but the Lacedaemonians and the Tegeans
put the barbarians to flight, while the Athenians and Plataeans successfully fought all the Greeks who had given up on freedom and sub-
47 mitted to slavery. On that day they put a perfect end to their earlier
dangers and secured the freedom of Greece. In all their encounters they
proved their virtue, fighting alone and with allies, both on foot and at
sea, against both barbarians and Greeks. Everybody — both the allies
with whom they took their chances and the enemy against whom they
fought — thought they deserved to be the leaders of Greece.

---

[44] See glossary under **born of the earth**.

[45] "Individual" is *idios*. See glossary under **public and private**.

[46] The battle of Plataea, in 479, put an end to the Persian campaign
against Greece (for a narrative see Herodotus 9.16–88). The Spartans
played a more important role than the Athenians. Although the funeral orations give Plataea a less prominent treatment than Marathon
and Salamis, others accounts give the success its proper due (see note
32 (p. 18) on Thucydides).

48   Later on, the Hellenic war arose out of envy and jealousy of the Athenians' earlier achievements.[47] Everybody was high spirited, and little cause was needed. In a sea battle against the Aeginetans and their
49 allies the Athenians captured seventy of their triremes. When they were besieging Egypt and Aegina at this same time, all of the youth were away from the city in the navy and the army. The Corinthians and their allies set out in full force and captured Geraneia, thinking that either they would invade an unprotected land or else that the Atheni-
50 ans would withdraw their army from Aegina. The Athenians didn't call upon any of their troops, from near or far. Because of their trust in their own spirits and contempt for the attackers, the older and the younger were prepared to undergo the risk alone. Some of them possessed virtue
51 based on experience, others based on nature.[48] The former had themselves already demonstrated their bravery everywhere,[49] and the latter imitated them. The older men knew how to command, and the younger
52 men were able to follow orders. With Myronides as general they made an expedition into Megara and defeated their entire force in battle, despite the fact that the Athenian soldiers were past their prime or not
53 yet capable. These men had dared to invade Attica, but the Athenians met them elsewhere and erected a trophy for the deed, which was excellent for them and disgraceful for the enemy. Some were no longer physically strong, others not yet, but both groups were strong in their souls. They returned to their own land with the greatest glory. Some went back to school and the others made plans for what was left to be done.
54   It's not easy for one man to recount each and every risk undertaken by so many men, or to describe all their achievements during that entire period of time. What speech, or length of time, or orator would be able
55 to relate the virtue of the men lying here? With great toil and famous struggles and brave risk-taking they made Greece free. They demonstrated the greatness of their fatherland by ruling the sea for seventy

---

[47] In this paragraph Lysias refers to several events of the early 450s, during the so called "pentekontaetia," or "50-year period," between the Persian Wars and the Peloponnesian War. Thucydides provides a condensed narrative of the entire period (1.89–117). Athenian involvement in Egypt, the war with Aegina, and the activity in Megara are narrated in 1.104–106.

[48] The constant use of antithetical constructions, in which two contrasted ideas are expressed in parallel terms, sometimes leads to forced expressions. Here Lysias is referring to the two age groups, young and old. The older men are brave because of their past experiences. The young men, lacking that sort of experience, are brave because of their nature (*physis*) alone.

[49] See glossary under **brave**.

56 years, by keeping their allies free from strife, and by not endorsing the slavery of the many to the few. They forced all men to honor equality, and they did not make their allies weak, but strong. They appeared to be so powerful that the great King no longer desired the possessions of others, but rather he surrendered some of his own and was fearful for
57 the rest.[50] No triremes sailed out at that time from Asia; no tyrant was established among the Greeks; no Greek city was enslaved by the barbarians. Their virtue extended a great deal of self-control and respect to all people.[51] For this reason they alone should lead the other cities as the foremost of the Greeks.

58   In their misfortunes they displayed virtue.[52] When our ships were destroyed at the Hellespont, whether because of the cowardice of the generals or the will of the gods, and the other Greeks joined us in the misfortune of that great disaster, it soon became clear that the power
59 of this city was the savior of Greece.[53] Then when others took over the leadership of Greece, those who had never before gone to sea conquered the Greeks at sea and sailed against Europe.[54] The Persians enslaved Greek cities and imposed tyrants, some after our misfortune,
60 others after the barbarian victory. Now at this grave we should cut our hair in mourning for Greece and grieve for those lying here, because Greek freedom lies buried with their virtue. Greece is unfortunate to be deprived of such men, while the King of Asia is lucky to find other leaders. Slavery awaits Greece now that these men are gone, while the King emulates his ancestors' plan now that others are in command.

61   I was brought here to make these laments for all of Greece. But we should remember these men both privately and publicly, since they

---

[50] The speaker is summarizing the entire period of the Delian League (see note 17 (p. 14) on Thucydides), from 478 to 404.

[51] Literally "a great deal of moderation (*sōphrosynē*) and fear (*deos*)." *Sōphrosynē* refers to the discretion and opportunity to exercise good judgment which Athenian protection provided to the other Greeks.

[52] On the euphemism see note 39 (p. 35) above.

[53] The battle of Aegospotami occurred near the Hellespont in 405. The Athenian navy was pursuing the Spartan fleet, which had successfully besieged the nearby city of Lampsacus. The Athenians tried to force a confrontation, but the Spartans held a superior position until eventually they took the Athenians by surprise and captured 140 of their 160 ships and killed all those aboard. For an account see Xenophon, *Hellenica* 2.1.17–32.

[54] The Persian fleet, under the leadership of the Athenian general Conon, defeated the Spartans at Cnidus in 395. Conon had escaped from Aegospotami (see note 53 (p. 39) above) and been living in Cyprus. He was eager to undermine Spartan supremacy after his earlier defeat at their hands. See Xenophon, *Hellenica* 4.3.10–14.

fled from slavery and fought for justice, when they stood up for democracy and went to the Piraeus despite so much hostility.[55] They were
persuaded by their nature, not compelled by law, and in these recent
62 battles they imitated the ancient virtue of their ancestors. With their
lives they opened up the city for others to share in. They chose death
with freedom over a life in slavery, because they were no less ashamed
of their misfortune than angry at their enemies, and they preferred dying in their own land to living as a resident of another's. They had
oaths and agreements for their allies, but in addition to their former
63 enemies, they also had their fellow-citizens. They were not afraid of
the number of the enemy, instead they exposed themselves to danger
and established a trophy over the enemy. They left the tomb for the
Lacedaemonians, close to this memorial, as a witness to their virtue.[56]
They showed that the city was great, not small, and they revealed that
it were unified, not divided, and they put up walls in place of those that
64 had been taken down.[57] Those who returned revealed a policy akin to
the deeds of those lying here. They did not attend to the punishment
of their enemy, but to the salvation of the city. They could not be defeated, but they didn't desire more acquisitions. They gave a share of
their freedom to those who had consented to being slaves, although they
65 had refused to have any part in their slavery.[58] Their great acts of brav-

---

[55] In this paragraph Lysias refers to the events at the end of the Peloponnesian War. The so-called "thirty tyrants" were installed at Athens
with Spartan support in 404. These officials suspended many democratic institutions and proscribed leading citizens and foreigners. Many
democrats resisted and went into exile at the Athenian port of Piraeus.
These democrats defeated the thirty in battle in early 403 and democracy was reinstituted in fall of that year. Amnesty was declared for all
but the thirty themselves. Lysias' account here is tempered by that
amnesty to some extent, but it is natural that he is unwilling to elaborate on these misfortunes in a speech at such a solemn occasion. In
Speech 12, *Against Eratosthenes*, he attacks one of the thirty for killing
his brother and provides a vivid portrait of the thirty's reign of terror.
Aristotle (*Constitution of the Athenians* 34–41.1) and Xenophon (*Hellenica* 2.3.10–2.4.43) provide accounts of the thirty. Krentz 1982 offers
a good modern account.

[56] A tomb for the Lacedaemonian officers who died in the confrontation
of 403 is located in the northwest region of the Ceramicus cemetery.

[57] Conon used Persian funds to rebuild the walls in 394 (Xenophon, *Hellenica* 4.8.10).

[58] Slaves who participated in the defeat of the tyrants may have been rewarded with citizenship, according to one interpretation of a fragmen-
tary inscription (Harding 1985, no. 3). But Lysias refers more generally
to the Athenian citizens who remained in Athens during the reign of the

ery proved that the city's earlier bad luck was not due to cowardice on their part or to any virtue on the part of the enemy. Although they were violently at odds with each other when the Peloponnesians and other enemies were here in their land, they were still able to return.[59] Clearly, if they were unified they would easily be able to fight the enemy.

66   Those men were envied by all mankind because of the dangers they faced in the Piraeus. The allies buried here also deserve to be praised, since they came to the aid of the people and fought for our city.[60] Because they believed virtue to be their fatherland, they died in such a way. This city mourns them and buries them at public expense, granting them the same honors as the citizens for all eternity.

67   These men now being buried came to the aid of the Corinthians by becoming their new allies when they were wronged by their former friends.[61] These men did not have the same attitude as the Lacedaemonians: the Lacedaemonians were jealous of the Corinthians' goods, whereas we pitied the fact that the Corinthians were being wronged, and we did not dwell upon previous hostility, but instead considered the present alliance to be of the utmost importance. Thus, these men **68** displayed their virtue to all mankind. To make Greece great, they were willing to jeopardize their own safety and to die for the freedom of their enemy. That is to say, they fought the allies of the Lacedaemonians for the freedom of Lacedaemonian allies. If they had won they would have given them freedom, but in their defeat they left behind slavery for the **69** Peloponnesians. For men in that condition life is pitiful and death is a prayer. But these men are to be envied both in their life and in death, because they were schooled in the good qualities of their ancestors, and as adults they preserved the glory of those generations and displayed **70** their own virtue. They have been the cause of much good for their fatherland, and they recovered what was lost by others and kept the war far away.

Thirty.

[59] Lysias is referring to the return of the exiled democrats from the Piraeus to Athens.

[60] Hyperides (11) refers to foreign mercenaries who fought alongside the Athenian forces and Thucydides (34.4 and 36.4) refers to their participation in the burial ceremony. Loraux 1986, 32–37 discusses the uncertain possibility that foreign remains were included with the Athenians in the public monument.

[61] In the Corinthian War (395–386) the Athenians joined with the cities of Thebes, Corinth and Argos to oppose the Spartans, who were supreme in Greece after the end of the Peloponnesian War. Important battles occurred at sea at Cnidus (note 54 (p. 39) above,) and on land near Corinth. See Xenophon, *Hellenica*, 3.5.1–2 on the alliance and books 4–5 for a narrative of the war itself.

They have ended their lives just as brave men must: they have repaid their debt to their fatherland and left behind grief for their parents.[62] Now the living will long for them and lament their own misfortune and pity the relatives of the dead as long as they live. What pleasure still remains for the living after men of such greatness are buried, men who deprived themselves of life because they regarded everything as inferior to virtue, men who made their wives widows, men who left behind their children to be orphans, men who left their brothers, mothers and fathers in solitude? Despite the many hardships I envy their children, who are too young to know what sort of fathers they have lost, but I pity those from whom they were born, because they are too old to forget their own misfortune. What would be more painful than this: to bear and rear and bury your own children, to be weak with old age, to be friendless and resourceless, without any hope, to be pitied now by the same men who envied you before, to desire death more than life? The braver they were, the more grief there is for those who are left. When should they end their grief?[63] When the city struggles? But that's the time for others also to remember these men. In times of public good fortune? But there's good reason for grief, when one's children are dead and the living prosper from their virtue. In times of personal risks, when they see their former friends running away from them in need, and they see their enemies elevated by their misfortunes? I think we owe this one debt to the men lying here, that we honor their parents in the same way they did, and that we welcome their children as if we ourselves were their fathers, and that we be the sort of help for their wives that they were while alive.[64] What men would we more rightly honor than these lying here? Whom of the living would we justly consider more important than their relatives, who had the same amount of enjoyment from their virtue as anyone else, but who alone genuinely feel the misfortune now that they are dead?

I don't know why I should lament these sorts of things. We know that we are mortals once and for all. So then, why should we now be pained by things which we have long expected? Why should we bear these natural misfortunes as such a burden, when we know that death is shared by the worst men and the best men? Death does not overlook the wicked or admire the good, but it comes to all with equality. If it were possible for those who escape the dangers of war to be immortal for the future, it would be appropriate for the living to mourn the dead for all time. But as it is, nature is inferior to illnesses and old age, and the god who controls our fate is implacable. So we should

---

[62] On the address to the family see note 41 (p. 20) on Thucydides.

[63] This series of rhetorical questions and rejected answers is echoed by Hyperides (30).

[64] On care for the dead's children and parents see note 72 (p. 61) on Plato.

consider these men most blessed, since they risked everything for the greatest and most noble causes and ended their lives in this pursuit. They did not entrust themselves to chance or wait for a natural death, but instead they chose the most noble one. The memorials for them

80 are ageless, and their honors are the envy of all mankind.[65] They are mourned as mortals because of their nature, but they are celebrated as immortals because of their virtue. They are buried at public expense and contests of strength and wisdom and wealth have been instituted for them because those who die in war deserve to be honored in the

81 same way as the immortal gods. I for my part admire and envy them for their death, and I suppose that the only men for whom life is worthwhile are those who, after they receive mortal bodies, leave behind an immortal memory of their virtue. But nevertheless we must observe the ancient practice and lament the men being buried in accord with the ancestral custom.

---

[65] "Ageless" memorials are a common motif: compare Thucydides 43.2, Demosthenes 32, Hyperides 42.

Introduction

Plato was born in 427 and lived until 348. He was the most famous student of Socrates, and nearly all of his writing took the form of conversations in which his teacher serves as the protagonist. Plato opened his Academy as a school of philosophy in Athens after 388. Unlike Gorgias and the other Sophists, Plato regarded rhetoric as at best a sort of candy-coating for real knowledge,[1] and he did not regard rhetoric as a worthwhile pursuit in its own right. Rather than teach clever speaking, Plato's dialogues treat issues such as the nature of piety or justice (the *Euthyphro* and *Republic*).

Plato has incorporated a full funeral oration in his dialogue *Menexenus* (the entire work is translated here). Although Socrates had been convicted and executed by his fellow Athenians in 399, the historical detail in the speech indicates that it was written after 386, after the Corinthian War and Lysias' funeral oration.[2] Socrates presents a funeral oration by Aspasia, the well-known mistress of Pericles (see note 13 (p. 48) below). With the ascription to Aspasia, and also verbal echoes, the speech clearly looks back to a funeral oration by Pericles. Plato may well have read Thucydides' version, but he was certainly too young to see Pericles himself speak and must have relied on some secondhand account of the speech.[3] The frequent echoes of the funeral oration in Thucydides indicate that Plato has Pericles' speech of 431 in mind, whether he knew it from Thucydides or another source.[4] More generally Plato probably invokes Pericles as the most famous statesman of the previous generation. Pericles' well known relationship with Aspasia may have also appealed to Plato; it allows him to cast Aspasia in a similar role to Diotima in the *Symposium*.

Scholars differ in their interpretation of the dialogue. One reading sees the speech as an antagonistic response to Thucydides' idealized

---

[1] *Gorgias* 463e–466a; the *Phaedrus* is also concerned with oratory and rhetoric.

[2] Section 245e refers to the peace of 386. Other dialogues contain similar anachronisms. For example, the *Symposium* (182b) refers to the King's Peace of 387/386, although the dialogue is set in 416.

[3] Some see Plato's reference to Antiphon (236a), who was said to have been Thucydides' teacher, as a direct reference back to Thucydides.

[4] It's less likely that Plato is thinking of Pericles' speech of 439 (see p. 5 on this oration). For echoes, compare Plato 238d and Thucydides 37.1; Plato 239a and Thucydides 35.1; Plato 246e and Thucydides 42.4.

view of Athenian democracy under Pericles.[5] Elsewhere Plato criticizes Pericles, among others, for using rhetoric to please the people in the Assembly without actually teaching them to be good citizens (*Gorgias* 502d–504e). In the *Menexenus*, according to this interpretation, Plato praises Athens as he thinks it should be praised, with an emphasis on the aristocratic nature of the government (238d–239a). This reading also acknowledges the genuine earnestness of the *paramythia*, and points out allusions to tenets of Platonic philosophy.[6] Others see the funeral oration in the *Menexenus* as a sort of parody that adopts an ironical tone and exaggerates the faults of contemporary rhetoric, as seen by Plato.[7] The attention Plato gives to wars of Greeks against Greeks (242a–244b; see also p. 28 above) may be a critical counterpoint to the idealized Athens described earlier in the speech, and the attribution to Aspasia implies a criticism of not just Pericles, but many other prominent politicians who are said to have learned from her (235e).

---

234 SOCRATES: Are you coming from the marketplace, Menexenus, or where?

MENEXENUS: Yes, Socrates, from the marketplace, from the council building.

SOC.: What in particular took you to the council building? I see that you think you've reached the end of your education and of philosophy. Since you think you are already capable in that area, you now intend to turn to bigger things. Will you attempt to rule us

b   old men, my dear man, at your age, so that your household may continue to provide a caretaker for us?

MEN.: If you permit and advise me to rule, Socrates, I will be ready. If not, then I won't. Just now I was at the council building because I learned that the council is going to choose who will speak over the dead.[8] You know that they are about to hold a burial.

SOC.: Oh yes, whom did they choose?

MEN.: Nobody, they postponed the matter until tomorrow. I think Archinus or Dion will be chosen.[9]

---

[5] Kahn 1963.

[6] For example, the nature of virtue in 246e.

[7] Coventry 1989.

[8] The only other passage (Demosthenes, *On the Crown* 285) that refers to the mechanics of the process for selecting the orator refers to the "people" (*dēmos*), which usually indicates the assembly (*ekklēsia*), not the council (*boulē*).

[9] Archinus was associated with Thrasybulus, the leader of the democrat faction under the thirty tyrants, and participated in the restoration of the democracy in 403 (Aristotle, *Constitution of the Athenians* 34.3

c SOC.: You know, Menexenus, I think dying in war is probably a fine thing everywhere. The dead man gets a fine and magnificent burial, even if he died as a poor man. Even if he was a common man, he receives the praise of wise men. And their praise is not off-hand; their speeches are carefully prepared. They praise the dead so well

235 that they bewitch our souls by referring to the qualities present and lacking in each case, adorning the facts most beautifully with their words. They eulogize the city in every manner, by praising those who have died in battle, all of our ancestors who came before, and us who are still living. As a result, Menexenus, when I am praised

b by them, I feel very nobly treated and each time I listen I become tricked into thinking that I have immediately become greater and more noble and more fine. Foreign guests sometimes come along with me and they hear all these things and I immediately become more respectable in their eyes.[10] They seem to me to experience the same effect both with regard to me and the others parts of the city: they believe that it is more excellent than before, because they have been influenced by the speaker. And that sense of dignity remains

c with me for more than three days. Such stirring speech and sound enters from the speaker into my ears that on the fourth or fifth day I barely come to my senses and understand where in the world I am. Until then I almost think I dwell on the islands of the blessed.[11] That's how clever our orators are.

MEN.: You always tease the orators, Socrates. But I expect the chosen speaker will not be well prepared, since the selection is happening very suddenly, so that the speaker will probably be forced to improvise.[12]

d SOC.: How come? Each of those orators has prepared speeches, and, in any case it is not very difficult to improvise that sort of thing. Praise of Athenians before Peloponnesians, or of Peloponnesians before Athenians, would require a good orator who is persuasive

---

and 40.1–2). An Athenian Dion, who is named by Xenophon as an ambassador to Persia in 392 (*Hellenica* 4.8.13), is more likely to be under consideration by the council than his more famous namesake from Syracuse.

[10] See note 60 (p. 41) on Lysias for other references to non-Athenians in attendance at the burials.

[11] The islands of the blessed, also known as the Elysian Field, were home only to a select few in the afterlife, who lived with the Olympian gods at the edge of the Earth. See Homer, *Odyssey* 4.563–569, Hesiod, *Works and Days* 168–173, Pindar, *Olympian* 2.70ff. Demosthenes (34) also refers to the dead in the islands of the blessed, while Hyperides (35–38) refers to the dead in Hades, the underworld.

[12] On the short notice given to the orators, see note 9 (p. 28) on Lysias.

and pleasing. But when a speaker contends before those whom he
also praises, it's no great feat to appear to speak well.

MEN.: You don't think so, Socrates?

SOC.: No, by Zeus.

e MEN.: What if the council were to choose you and you had to speak?
Do you think you could do it?

SOC.: It's not surprising that I would be able to speak, Menexenus,
since I happen to have no ordinary teacher of rhetoric. She has also
made many other men into good orators, including the foremost of
the Greeks, Pericles the son of Xanthippus.

MEN.: Who is she? I suppose you mean Aspasia.[13]

SOC.: I do, and also Connon the son of Metrobius.[14] These are my two
236 teachers, the one in music, the other in rhetoric. It's no surprise
that one trained in such a manner is clever at speaking. But let's
consider someone trained more commonly than me, in music by
Lamprus and in rhetoric by Antiphon of Rhamnus.[15] Even that
man would be able to look good when praising Athenians before
Athenians.

MEN.: What would you have to say, if you were required to speak?

b SOC.: I might not have anything of my own, but just yesterday I heard
Aspasia reciting a funeral oration for these very men. She heard
about that business you just mentioned, that the Athenians were
about to choose a speaker. She then went through the sort of things
one should say, improvising some parts and patching in other left-
over bits she had prepared earlier, when, I think, she composed the
funeral oration which Pericles delivered.

MEN.: Could you remember what Aspasia said?

SOC.: As long as I don't make a mistake. I learned it from her and she
c all but beat me when I forgot anything.[16]

MEN.: Why don't you go through it?

SOC.: I hope my teacher won't mind if I publish her speech.

---

[13] Aspasia of Miletus was the mistress of Pericles. She was connected
with Socrates by contemporary writers such as Xenophon (*Memora-
bilia* 2.6.36 and *Oeconomicus* 3.14) and Socrates' follower Aeschines,
and also in later accounts, such as Plutarch, *Pericles* 24–25. For a modern study of the ancient evidence see Henry 1995.

[14] Plato also refers to Connon, Socrates' music teacher, at *Euthydemus*
272c.

[15] Lamprus was a fifth-century musician said in later times to have been
a teacher of Sophocles (Athenaeus, *Deipnosophists* 1.37). Antiphon of
Rhamnus was an Athenian orator, some of whose speeches survive, and
probably also the same Antiphon who wrote philosophical works.

[16] At *Phaedrus* 228a–e Plato introduces a similar reported speech, by the
orator Lysias, with a discussion of the process of memorization.

MEN.: Don't worry about that, Socrates, just speak. You will please
me greatly, if you are willing to recite Aspasia's speech or anything
else. Just speak.

SOC.: Perhaps you'll laugh at me, if I, at my age, appear to you to still
be playing.

MEN.: Not at all, Socrates, but by all means speak.

d   SOC.: Well, I suppose I must please you. If you were to command me
to strip and dance I would almost oblige you, since we are alone.
Please listen. She spoke, I think, beginning her speech with the
dead themselves like this:

"With acts these men have received their due from us,[17] and, now
that they have those honors, they are traveling along their fated jour-
ney, after a public procession from the city, and a private one from their
relatives.[18] However, the law requires us to pay off the honor that is still

e   owed to these men with a speech too, and it is right. A well-delivered
speech about noble deeds conveys memory and honor to the deeds' per-
formers from the listeners.[19] We require a speech that will sufficiently
praise the dead, and will graciously encourage the living, by enjoining
their children and brothers to imitate the virtue of these men, and by
consoling their fathers and mothers and any of their older ancestors still

237 left. Can we find a speech of that sort? Where should we rightly begin praising brave men,[20] who while living delighted their friends and
family with virtue,[21] and who traded their death for the safety of the
living? I think I should praise them according to the natural order, since
they were naturally good. They were good because they were born from
good men. Let's first eulogize their nobility of birth, and second their

b   upbringing and education. After these things let's look at the execu-
tion of their deeds, such a noble and deserving display. First of all, the
fact that the origin of their ancestors was not foreign was the source of
their nobility.[22] It showed that their descendants were not transplants
to this land with ancestors who had come from elsewhere, but rather
that they were born of the earth and that they really dwelled and lived
in their fatherland, and that they were not nourished by a step-mother,

c   as others were, but by the motherland in which they lived, which had

---

17 The "acts" are the funeral games that preceded the oration. The
speaker contrasts these with the "speech" in the next sentence. See
glossary under **speech and deeds**.

18 For the details of the burial ceremony see Thucydides 34.1–6.

19 At this point other orators typically express worry about their speech
being inferior to the accomplishments of the dead. See note 6 (p. 64)
on Demosthenes.

20 See glossary under **brave**.

21 See glossary under **virtue**.

22 See note 15 (p. 13) on Thucydides on the *genos* as a topic of praise.

given birth to them and raised them and received them back to rest in death.[23] It is most just to honor first their mother herself, and at the same time we will honor the nobility of these men too.

    All mankind, not we alone, ought to praise this region, for many reasons, but first and most especially because it happens to be favored by the gods. The strife and judgment of the gods in their dispute over d it will confirm my statement.[24] Isn't it right that all mankind praise the land which the gods praise? Secondly, it deserves praise because at that time, when the whole earth was giving birth and bearing all sorts of animals, carnivorous and vegetarian beasts, at that time our region appeared childless and pure with no wild beasts. Then it chose out of the animals and gave birth to mankind, who stands above the e others in intelligence and alone believes in justice and the gods. The fact that this land gave birth to the ancestors of these men and ourselves is a great proof of this statement. Everything that gives birth provides suitable nourishment for its offspring, and this criterion reveals whether a woman is truly a mother or not, if she does not have sources of nourishment for her offspring. Our land and mother provides this as sufficient proof that it gave birth to humans.[25] It was the only one at that time and the first to bear as human nourishment the fruit 238 of wheat and barley, excellent nourishment for the human race, because it really gave birth to this creature. This kind of proof is more valid for the earth than for a woman, since the earth does not imitate a woman in conception and birth, but a woman imitates the earth. She was not stingy with this produce and she distributed it to others too. After this b she saw to the birth of the olive for her children, an aid for work. After raising them and bringing them up to adolescence, she introduced the gods as rulers and teachers for them. I should pass over their names in this sort of a speech — we know them.[26] They prepared them for day-to-day life by teaching them fundamental skills and by instructing

---

[23] See glossary under **born of the earth**.

[24] Herodotus (8.55) refers to the contest between Athena and Poseidon for Attica.

[25] Despite the fact that the land was in fact not very fertile and they relied on imports, the Athenians were proud of their local produce, especially the olive, thought of as a gift from Athena (see, for example, Sophocles, *Oedipus at Colonus* 668–719) and grain, a gift from Demeter, given along with the knowledge of agriculture to the mythical prince Triptolemus (the subject of a famous play by Sophocles, surviving only in fragments).

[26] Mourners were polluted by their association with the dead and were prevented from entering holy places or even naming the Olympian deities (Parker 1983, 64–65). See also Demosthenes 30, where the orator refuses to name the god Dionysus.

them in the possession and use of weapons to protect the land.

The ancestors of these men were born and educated in that fashion. They furnished a government for themselves and lived with it, and
c I would like to describe it briefly. Government is the nourishment of mankind:[27] a noble government for good men and the opposite for vile men. I must show that those who came before us were raised with a good government, and because of that government both the men of old and we today are good, and these men who have died happen to be part of that group. The government was the same then and now, the rule of the best, and we still administer our city just as we always have since that period, for the most part. One man calls it a democracy, another
d calls it something else, whatever he likes, but in truth it is an aristocracy with the approval of the majority.[28] We always have rulers, but these are sometimes hereditary and sometimes chosen. For the most part the majority is in charge of the city. They give offices and authority to whomever seems best to them at a particular time and nobody is excluded because of weakness or poverty or the obscurity of their fathers. We also do not honor anyone for the opposite reasons, as in other cities. There is one standard: the one who seems to be wise or good has power
e and rules. The fact that we were born on an equal footing is responsible for this government of ours. Other cities have been established by men of all kinds and various sorts, so that their governments also are varied; some are tyrannies, some oligarchies. Some of them live regarding each other as slaves, some as masters. But we and our people, since we
239 are born as brothers from one mother, do not regard ourselves as slaves or even masters of each other. Instead our equality of birth by nature compels us to seek equality by law and to yield to each other in nothing except reputation for virtue and judgment.[29]

It follows that the fathers of these men and ourselves, and these men themselves, were raised in complete freedom and nobly born. They displayed many fine achievements to all mankind both in private and
b in public, when they thought that they should fight for freedom against Greeks on behalf of Greeks, and against foreigners on behalf of all the Greeks.[30] There is not enough time to narrate how, when Eumolpus and the Amazons and their predecessors were campaigning against this land,[31] they defended themselves, and how they defended the Argives

---

[27] See glossary under **constitution**.

[28] For other descriptions of Athenian democracy see note 21 (p. 15) on Thucydides.

[29] On Athenian respect for the law, see note 22 (p. 15) on Thucydides.

[30] Plato now begins a typical narrative of the accomplishments of the Athenians. Compare Lysias 3–66 and Demosthenes 6–11, and see also note 18 (p. 14) on Thucydides.

[31] Eumolpus was a legendary king of Thrace who led the Eleusinians to

from the Cadmeans,[32] and the children of Heracles from the Argives.[33] And the poets have already well praised the virtue of these men in their

c songs and left a memorial for all.[34] If we attempt to honor the same acts in prose we would probably place second.[35] For these reasons I am inclined to pass over this material, since it has already received its due praise. But there is still worthwhile material, which no poet has used to build a reputation and which is still uncelebrated. I think I must relate these matters, and in doing so I will praise these men myself and I will also provide material for others to use in their songs and other types of poetry, as befits the men who performed these deeds.

d Here are the first of those matters I am addressing. The descendants of this land, our fathers, restrained the Persians, who were ruling Asia and enslaving Europe, and it is both just and right to remember this first and praise their virtue.[36] If one wants to praise them properly, their virtue ought to be examined by setting the speech at the time when all of Asia was already enslaved to the third king. The first king,

e Cyrus, boldly freed his fellow citizens, the Persians, and at the same time enslaved their masters, the Medes, and ruled the rest of Asia as far as Egypt.[37] His son ruled Egypt and Libya, as far as he could reach. The third king, Darius, extended the empire with his army as far as

240 Scythia, and with his navy he commanded the sea and the islands such that nobody wanted to be his adversary. The minds of all mankind were enslaved. The Persian empire reduced so many great and fierce nations to slavery.

Darius charged us and the Eretrians on the pretext that we had

---

fight against the Athenians. The Athenian king Erechtheus sacrificed his daughters, at the behest of the oracle at Delphi, in order to defeat Eumolpus. Euripides' *Erechtheus* included these events (the play is mostly lost, but a speech of Erechtheus' wife, Praxithea, is quoted at Lycurgus, *Against Leocrates* 100). On the Amazons see note 15 (p. 29) on Lysias. These mythical events briefly referred to here are divided into offensive and defensive successes.

[32] For the Seven against Thebes see note 18 (p. 30) on Lysias.

[33] On the children of Heracles see note 23 (p. 31) on Lysias.

[34] See note 32 (p. 18) on Thucydides on poems for the dead.

[35] Demosthenes (9) also refers to earlier poetic accounts celebrating the accomplishments of Athens, which he distinguishes from praise in prose. Thucydides rejects these poetic accounts (41.4).

[36] On the Persian Wars see note 28 (p. 33) on Lysias.

[37] Cyrus the Great (ruled c. 557–530) oversaw the creation of the Persian Empire. His son Cambyses (ruled 530–522) brought Egypt under Persian control. Darius seized power after Cambyses' death and held it until his own death in 486. The early books of Herodotus' *Histories* narrate the growth of the Persian Empire.

plotted against Sardis.[38] He sent out 500,000 men on sailing ships and triremes, with 300 fighting boats and Datis in command. Darius told Datis to bring back the Eretrians and the Athenians if he wanted to
b keep his own head. Datis sailed to Eretria to face men who were the most renowned fighters in Greece at that time and who were not few. He defeated them in three days and searched the whole region so that no one could escape, in this way: his soldiers went to the Eretrian borders and stood at intervals from coast to coast and, joining their hands
c together, they went through the whole area, so that they could tell the King that no one had escaped. They had the same plan as they went from Eretria to Marathon, and they took it for granted that they would bring back the Athenians under the same yoke of necessity as the Eretrians.[39] Despite these Persian achievements and attempts, none of the Greeks aided the Eretrians or the Athenians except the Lacedaemonians — but they arrived on the day after the battle. All the others were
d cowed and, preferring their immediate safety, they kept quiet. Anyone who was born in that time could recognize how virtuous they were, when at Marathon they met the force of the barbarians and punished the insolence of all Asia, and raised the first trophies over the barbarians. They were leaders and they taught others that the Persian force was not invincible, and that every multitude and every asset yields to
e virtue. I assert that those men were not just the fathers of our bodies, but also of our freedom, and the freedom of everyone on this continent. The Greeks looked at that deed and gained the courage to fight the later battles too for freedom as students of the men at Marathon.

241 This speech must give the first prize to those men, but the second prize goes to the ones who fought at sea and won at Salamis and Artemisium.[40] There is much to say about these men, and the sort of attacks they endured on land and sea, and how they defended themselves against these. I will mention one deed which seems to me to be their finest, since they did it next after Marathon. The men at Marathon
b demonstrated only this much: that it was possible for a few men to ward off many barbarians on land. But the Persian navy was still untested and they had the reputation of being invincible at sea because of their numbers and their wealth and their skill and their strength. The men in our navy at that time deserve praise for destroying the remaining

---

[38] The Athenians and Eretrians aided the eastern Greek cities who revolted from Darius and burned the Persian city of Sardis in 498 (see Herodotus 5.199–102). Darius' expedition of 490 was advertised as revenge for these earlier events. On the siege of Eretria see Herodotus 6.100–102.

[39] See note 29 (p. 33) on Lysias for the battle of Marathon. on the Spartans' tardiness see Herodotus 6.120.

[40] On these battles see note 40 (p. 36) and note 36 (p. 35) on Lysias.

fear of the Greeks and ending their terror at the multitude of ships and men. The other Greeks were educated by both the men in the army
c at Marathon and those in the navy at Salamis. They learned to become used to not fearing the barbarians on land or at sea. I count the work at Plataea for the safety of Greece third in number and virtue, and this one at last was shared between the Lacedaemonians and the Athenians.[41] All these men prevented the worst possible outcome, and because of this virtue they are now eulogized by us, and also in the
d future by those who come after us. After this many Greek cities were still on the side of the barbarians, and the King himself was said to be intending to attack Greece again. It is just that we mention those men too, who put the finishing touch on earlier achievements for our safety by clearing out and driving off all barbarity from our sea. These were
e the men who fought at sea at Eurymedon and those who campaigned at Cyprus and those who sailed to Egypt and many other places. We must remember them and thank them for making the King fearfully watch out for his own safety instead of planning the destruction of the Greeks.[42]

The whole city endured that war against the barbarians for our own
242 sake, and for the others who speak our language.[43] Afterward, there was peace and our city was honored. But then, as commonly happens when people are successful, it encountered envy at first, and then as a result of envy, jealousy. This also brought our city, against its will, into war with Greeks. After this, when the war occurred, we joined the fight against the Lacedaemonians in Tanagra for the freedom of the
b Boeotians.[44] Although that battle was indecisive, the event that followed made the determination. The others left, abandoning those they had come to aid, but our forces were victorious on the third day of battle at Oenophyta, and we justly restored those men who were wrongly exiled. Those men of ours, who were already fighting against Greeks for Greek freedom, were also the first ones after the Persian war to achieve

---

[41] On the battle of Plataea see note 46 (p. 37) on Lysias. Herodotus (9.71) observes that the Spartans were the most praise-worthy at that battle.

[42] In the battle of Eurymedon Athenian forces defeated the Persians in Asia Minor in 466 (Thucydides 1.100). The activity in Egypt and Cyprus took place between 461 and 458 (Thucydides 1.104). Lysias 48–53 also summarizes the history of this period (see note 47 (p. 38) on Lysias).

[43] See glossary under **barbarian**.

[44] According to Thucydides, the Spartans defeated the Athenians at Tanagra, a city in the region of Boeotia, northwest of Attica, in 457. Not long after the Athenians took over the area by defeating the Boeotians at Oenophyta (Thucydides 1.108).

c nobility and free those they were helping,[45] and they were the first ones placed in this memorial with honor by the city. After these events, widespread war continued and all the Greeks invaded and destroyed our territory, paying back an undeserved thanks to our city. But our forces conquered them at sea and captured their leaders, the Lacedaemonians, in Sphagia.[46] Our men could have killed them, but we spared

d them, and surrendered them and made peace, thinking it right to wage war against our own kin only to the point of victory (unlike barbarians, whom we must destroy), and not to destroy the community of a Greek city because of a private provocation. The men who who fought that war and are buried here ought to be praised for showing us the wrongness of any claim that others were superior to the Athenians in that war against the foreigners. They made this demonstration by excelling in

e war while Greece was in turmoil, and by defeating the foremost of the other Greeks. Their own allies in the previous defeat of the barbarians were now the ones they beat on their own.

After this peace there was a third war, unforeseen and savage.[47] Many brave men who died in that campaign are buried here. Many

243 sailed to Sicily and erected numerous victory trophies for the freedom of the Leontinians, when they sailed to that land as sworn allies. But because of the length of the voyage our city was helpless and unable to support the force, so we renounced this plan and suffered misfortune.[48] The enemies of these men and those who fought against them praised their moderation and virtue more than other peoples' friends do. Many of these men fought in the sea-battle at the Hellespont, where in one

b day they captured all the enemies' ships, and defeated many others.[49] When I said that the nature of that war was unforeseen and savage, I was referring to this: the other Greeks felt so much rivalry toward this city that they dared to send ambassadors to that most hateful King, whom they had helped to expel as our allies, and to bring that man back on their own, a barbarian against Greeks, and to assemble all the Greeks and barbarians against our city.[50] On that occasion the strength

---

[45] See glossary under **brave**.

[46] Sphagia, or Sphacteria, was an island just off the coast of Pylos in the southern Peloponnese, where in 425 the Athenians defeated and captured a Spartan force (Thucydides 4.2–41).

[47] Plato is referring to the second part of the Peloponnesian War, beginning with the unsuccessful Athenian expedition to Sicily (415–413).

[48] On this phrase see glossary under **chance** and note 39 (p. 35) on Lysias.

[49] Plato refers to events of 411–410, narrated by Thucydides (8.104–106).

[50] In 412 the Spartans made an agreement with the Persian king Tissaphernes to act together to thwart Athenian interests in Ionia. See Thucydides 8.36–37.

c and virtue of this city was plain to see. When the enemy thought we had been subdued by the war and that our ships were cut off at Mytilene, we sent sixty ships to help and these men manned the ships and indisputably achieved the utmost nobility on the field.[51] They conquered the enemy and freed their allies, but they encountered an undeserved fortune and they were not taken up from the sea for burial here.[52] We

d must always remember and praise those men. It is thanks to their virtue that we were victorious not only in that sea-battle then, but also in the rest of the war. Because of them our city acquired the reputation of being unbeatable by anybody. And it's true; we were overpowered by ruin at our own hands, not from others. Still even now we are undefeated by those men, but we have defeated ourselves and been defeated by ourselves.[53]

After these events, when our foreign affairs were calm and peaceful,

e our civil war was conducted such that no one would pray for his city to suffer this differently, if men are fated to engage in strife.[54] With great gladness and closeness the citizens from the Piraeus and from the city came to terms, not just with each other, but also, to our surprise, with the other Greeks. They conducted the war against those at Eleusis

244 with great moderation. For all this there was no other cause than their genuine kinship, which provided a firm and homogeneous relationship, not in word but in deed.[55] We must remember those who died at each other's hands in this war and reconcile them with what we have, prayers and sacrifices, at these sorts of occasions, by praying to those who look after them, since we ourselves have been reconciled. They attacked each other not because of evil or hatred, but because of misfortune.[56] We

b ourselves who are alive are witnesses to these events. We, who are the same as them by birth, forgive each other for what we did and what we suffered.

After this we had absolute peace and the city was calm. We forgave

---

[51] See glossary under **brave**.

[52] See glossary under **chance**. In 406 the Athenians defeated the Spartans in a naval battle near Arginusae, islands near Lesbos in the eastern Aegean. However the Athenian commanders did not retrieve the bodies of the dead for burial and were subsequently tried and executed. See Xenophon, *Hellenica* 1.7 for a detailed account of the trial of the generals.

[53] Similarly Lysias (31) and Demosthenes (19) refuse to describe the fallen as defeated by the enemy.

[54] On the events in Athens at the end of the Peloponnesian War see note 55 (p. 40) on Lysias. Many of the thirty tyrants took refuge in Eleusis after they were defeated by the democrats.

[55] See glossary under **speech and deeds**.

[56] See 243a above and note 39 (p. 35) on Lysias.

the barbarians, since their defense was not lacking when they suffered badly at our hands, but we were irritated with the Greeks. We remembered how they paid back the favor when they were well treated by
c   us, by associating with the barbarians, stripping away the ships which had once saved them, and taking down the walls in return for the fact that we had prevented theirs from falling. The city then decided that it would no longer defend the Greeks, whether they were being enslaved by each other or the barbarians, and it conducted itself accordingly. Since this was our attitude, the Lacedaemonians believed that we, the
d   allies of freedom, had fallen, and that it was their job to enslave others, and so they did.[57] But why should I go on at length? The things that came next which I might mention did not happen long ago and they are not the deeds of ancient men. We ourselves know that the foremost men of the Greeks, the Argives, the Boeotians and the Corinthians, stricken by fear, came to this city for help, and, most amazing of all, the King became so helpless that his safety happened to come from nowhere other than the city which he had sought to destroy.[58]

e   If anyone desires to accuse our city fairly, there's only one real accusation, that we are always too prone to pity and favor the underdog.[59] At that time our city was not able to persevere or abide by what it had
245 decided, not to rescue anybody who was being enslaved from those who were wronging them. It relented and went out to help. By coming to the aid of the Greeks it released them from slavery, and they remained free until they again enslaved themselves. Although it did not dare to aid the King, out of respect for the trophies at Marathon and Salamis and Plataea, it certainly did save him by allowing only exiles and vol-
b   unteers to help. After rebuilding our walls and restoring our navy it took up the war, once forced to fight, and fought the Lacedaemonians on behalf of the Parians.[60] The King feared the city after he saw the Lacedaemonians renouncing the war at sea and he wanted to desert the cause, so he demanded the continental Greeks, whom the Lacedaemonians had earlier surrendered to him, if he was going to fight alongside us and the other allies, thinking we would refuse and that he would have an

---

[57] On the Spartan hegemony and the Corinthian War see note 61 (p. 41) on Lysias.

[58] On the Athenian general Conon's cooperation with Persia see note 54 (p. 39) on Lysias.

[59] Plato casts recent events as a modern-day demonstration of Athenian willingness to aid suppliants. See note 23 (p. 31) on Lysias for mythical examples of this tradition. Frequently in this paragraph he personifies the city of Athens as the agent responsible for these deeds ("it").

[60] Plato continues to refer to the Athenian general Conon, who had been living abroad. See note 57 (p. 40) on the rebuilding of the walls. "Parians" is probably a mistake by Plato or a copyist for "Persians".

c excuse for his desertion. He was mistaken about the other allies. They were willing to give up the continental Greeks to him. The Corinthians and Argives and Boeotians and other allies agreed and swore that they would give up the continental Greeks if he would provide support. We alone dared not to surrender them or to swear the oath.[61]

The nobility and freedom of the city is so strong and healthy and
d anti-barbarian in nature because we are pure Greeks with no barbarian taint. No Pelops or Cadmus or Aegyptus or Danaus or any others who are barbarian in nature, but in custom Greek, dwell among us.[62] We live together as Greeks, with no half-barbarians, so that a pure hatred for foreign nature has been cast deep in this city.[63] Nevertheless, we
e were again alone because we were unwilling to perform the shameful and unholy act of surrendering Greeks to barbarians. Although we found ourselves in the same position as before, when we were defeated, with god's help we fought this war better than that one. We came out of the war with our ships, our walls, and our colonies, so well in fact that even our enemy was glad to be done with it.[64] But we lost brave men in this war too, who suffered from the bad terrain in Corinth and betrayal in
246 Lechaeum.[65] The men who freed the King and drove the Lacedaemonians from the sea were also brave. I remind you of those men and ask you to join me in praising and honoring their greatness.

Many fine words have been said about the achievements of the men lying here and all the others who died in war, but even so, many fine
b deeds have been omitted. Several days and nights would not be enough time for someone who intends to praise everything. Everyone should remember these men and advise their offspring, just as in war, not to leave the post of their forefathers or retreat by yielding to cowardice.[66]

---

[61] On these negotiations between Persia and the Greeks over Greek interests in Ionia, see Xenophon, *Hellenica* 4.8.12–17.

[62] These mythical heroes were associated with various lands. Pelops was the eponym of the Peloponnesian peninsula of the Greek mainland. Cadmus came from Phoenicia, in some accounts, to settle Thebes in Boeotia. Aegyptus was the namesake of the Egyptians. Danaus was Aegyptus' brother, who fled from Egypt to the city of Argos in the Peloponnese.

[63] The verb "cast" (*syntēkein*) is usually used to describe the molding of hot molten metals. "Pure" (*katharos*) reinforces the metaphor.

[64] The Persian king Artaxerxes ended the Persian War in 386 with the so-called "King's Peace" (Xenophon, *Hellenica* 5.1.29–31).

[65] See glossary under **brave**. Lechaeum was one of the ports of the city of Corinth. The Spartans captured the port by treachery in 392 and used it as a local base against the other Greek allies (Xenophon, *Hellenica* 4.4.7–14).

[66] On the address to the wives and parents in this section of the speech

For that reason I also advise you, the children of brave men, now and
c in the future, whenever I encounter any of you, and remind and exhort
you to strive to be as brave as possible. On this occasion it is right for
me to tell you what your fathers, as they were about to risk their lives,
commanded us to tell their survivors. I will tell you the very things
I heard them say, and also what they would happily say to you now
if they were able, making an inference from what they said then. But
you must believe that you are hearing whatever I say from those men
themselves. They spoke like this.

d   'Children, the present circumstance reveals that you are born of
brave fathers. Although we could stay alive as cowards, we prefer to
die bravely, without causing any disgrace for you and the next generation or any shame for all our ancestors. We believe that life is unlivable
for someone who shames his own family, and that no man or god is a
friend to such a man, either on the earth or below the earth when he
e dies. Listen to our speech and, whatever you pursue, pursue it with
virtue, with the awareness that all possessions and pursuits are shameful and evil without this. Wealth does not bring beauty to one who
possesses it with cowardice, because that sort of man's wealth belongs
to somebody else, not himself. Physical beauty and strength, dwelling
alongside cowardice and evil, are not attractive.[67] They are unattrac-
tive, and they make the bearer more conspicuous and reveal his cowardice. All knowledge, if devoid of justice and the rest of virtue, appears
247 as trickery, not wisdom. For this reason in the beginning and the end,
throughout all time and by all means, with all your eagerness strive to
surpass us and our ancestors in renown.[68] If not, know that for us, if
we are victorious over you in virtue, the victory brings shame, whereas
the defeat, if we are defeated, brings blessedness. We would be most
defeated and you would be victorious, if you are prepared not to abuse
b the glory of your forefathers nor to squander it away, because you know
that nothing is more shameful for a man who supposes he is somebody
than to be honored not on his own account, but because of the glory of
his ancestors. The fact that one's parents have honors is a beautiful and
noble treasure for their descendants. But it is shameful and cowardly

---

see note 41 (p. 20).

[67] Plato here echoes Thucydides 42.2. See note 35 (p. 18) on Thucydides.

[68] "Throughout all time and by all means, strive to have total ...": a
striking example of polyptoton, or repetition of the same word in different usages. The Greek reads *pantos pasan pantōs*, repeating the same
word for "all" three times. Rhetorical figures such as these were especially popularized by the orator Gorgias, who was also fond of parallel
antithetical phrases, sometimes with emphatic repetition, such as in the
close repetition of "victory", "defeat" and "conquer" in the next two
sentences. See also note 11 (p. 25) on Gorgias.

to consume a treasure of money or honor, and not hand it on to one's children because of a lack of individual possessions and good sense of c one's own. But if you behave like this, you will come to us as friends to friends when your own fate brings you here. But if you neglect these things and are cowardly, no one will welcome you warmly. Please say these things to our children.

'We should always console our fathers and mothers, those of us that still have them, so that they may bear their misfortune, if that's what is, as easily as possible and not lament together.[69] They will not need any d more grief, since this present misfortune has provided enough of this. To heal and soothe them we should remind them that the gods have heard the greatest of their prayers. They did not pray that their children be immortal, but brave and renowned, and they got these things, which are the greatest goods. Having all one's prayers answered in life isn't easy for a mortal man to bear in his mind. But by bearing their misfortunes courageously they will truly appear to be the fathers of courageous chil- e dren and they themselves will appear to be courageous. But by giving in they will arouse suspicion, either that they are not our parents, or that those of us who praise them were deceived. Neither of these should be the case. Rather, they should praise us with their acts, by showing that they are real men and fathers of men. That old saying "nothing in excess" seems to be well said.[70] And it really is well said. If a man has 248 everything that contributes to happiness in his own hands, or nearly so, and he is not joined to other men such that his situation is also forced to fluctuate according to whether those men are doing well or badly, then that man has best prepared his life, and he is moderate, brave and in- telligent. When possessions and children are born and die, he will heed that proverb. He will not appear too happy or pained because he trusts b in himself. We ask, and desire, and tell our friends to be like this, and we now provide ourselves as examples, not being too upset or too afraid if we must die presently. We ask our fathers and mothers to lead the rest of their lives with the same attitude, and to know that they will not please us very much by bewailing and lamenting us. If there is any per- c ception of the living among the dead, they will displease us greatly by being distressed and bearing their misfortunes badly. But they would most please us by bearing it lightly and moderately. The end of our lives will be very noble for mankind, and praise will be more appropri- ate than mourning. But if they take care of our wives and children and

---

[69] Hyperides, in his consolatory address to the children of the fallen (27), similarly doubts their misfortune.

[70] "Nothing in excess" (*mēden agan*) and "know thyself" (*gnōthi seauton*) were inscribed at the Greek oracle of Delphi. Elsewhere (*Charmides* 164c–165b) Plato discusses these two admonitions and their relation to the Greek value of "moderation" (*sōphrosynē*).

nourish them and pay attention to that goal, they will probably forget their fortune and live more nobly and rightly with our approval.[71]

d   That's enough to tell our family and friends from us. We would encourage the city to take care of our fathers and sons for us, by teaching the latter decently, and by nursing the former in their old age as they deserve. But we know that even without our encouragement, you will take proper care of them.'

That's what they told us to report to you, the children and parents of the dead, and I am reporting it as enthusiastically as I can. I
e   myself also have a request on their behalf, that the sons imitate their own fathers, and that the parents have self-confidence, because we will nurse and care for you both in private and public, whenever any of us encounters anyone of them at all.[72] You yourselves are aware of the diligence of the city, and that it has enacted laws that the children and parents of the dead be cared for, and that the highest city official has
249 been appointed above all other citizens to see to it that the fathers and mothers of these men are not treated wrongly. The city itself helps raise their children, striving to make their orphanage insignificant by putting itself in the role of father for the ones who are still children.[73] After they reach manhood, it sends them off to their own responsibilities, after equipping them with full armor and reminding them of their
b   fathers' habits by giving them the tools of their paternal virtue. With good omens it sends them out, decorated in arms, to begin the strong rule of their father's home. It never stops honoring the dead. Each year we publicly observe the same customs for everyone that each receives in private.[74] In addition, the city enacts competitions in gymnastics, horses and all sorts of music. Simply put, it takes on the fated role of

---

[71] See glossary under **chance**.

[72] Greek culture placed a high value on children caring for their parents. The laws of the Archaic Athenian law-giver Solon required sons to care for their elderly fathers (Aristotle, *Constitution of the Athenians* 55.3). The state also acted in the role of parent for the orphaned children of the dead (see Harding 1985, no. 8). When they were old enough to begin military training, the orphans were given arms and they paraded at the City Dionysia, an annual religious festival which featured dramatic productions. See also Thucydides 46.1, Lysias 75, Demosthenes 32 and Hyperides 42. Goldhill 1990, 105–114 discusses the state's assumption of family roles. Monoson 2000, 181–205 emphasizes the importance of family relationships in this oration, which she sees as a reaction to the relationship between the state and the citizen described in Thucydides' oration. Although she is right in seeing that this speech directly replies to Pericles, some of the connections she draws are unconvincing.

[73] On the personification of the city see note 59 (p. 57) above.

[74] See glossary under **public and private**.

c   heir and son for the dead, and of father for sons, of guardian for their
     parents, and it takes complete care of all of them for all time.[75] You
     should take those facts to heart and bear your misfortune more lightly.
     In this way you would be more beloved to the dead and the living and
     it would be most easy for you to care and be cared for. But now that
     you and all the others have lamented the dead publicly according to the
     law, depart."
d   That's the speech of Aspasia of Miletus for you.
     MEN.: I must congratulate Aspasia, if she is able to compose such
         speeches despite being a woman.
     SOC.: If you don't believe it, come along with me and hear her speak
         yourself.
     MEN.: I've run into Aspasia many times and I know what she's like.
     SOC.: So then, don't you admire her and aren't you now thankful to
         her for this speech?
     MEN.: I am very thankful for this speech, either to her, or to him,
e   whoever it was who said it to you. And I am especially grateful
         to you for delivering it.
     SOC.: That's wonderful. Please don't give me away, and I will report
         many good political speeches from her to you.[76]
     MEN.: Don't worry, I won't tell on you. Just keep reporting them.
     SOC.: I will.

---

[75] Another case of polyptoton, with repetition of the same word, *pas*, or
     "all", three times. See note 68 (p. 59) above.
[76] "Political speeches" refers to any speeches relevant to the affairs of the
     city, or *polis*, which might include not only formal public speeches such
     as this one, but also speeches delivered in the Assembly or the courts on
     more specific questions of government. Perhaps there is an allegation
     that Aspasia was also behind other orations delivered by Pericles.

Introduction

Demosthenes was born to a wealthy Athenian family in 384. He first came to prominence in 364, when he prosecuted his guardians for mismanagement of his father's estate. There are anecdotes about Demosthenes developing a powerful delivery style by practicing his declamation with a mouthful of pebbles, or amid the noise of the waves at the seashore.[1] After the success of his early prosecution against his guardians, Demosthenes earned a living like Lysias, as a writer of speeches for clients to use in court. Eventually, in the mid 350s, he began to give speeches in the public assembly, many of which survive today. He became famous for his opposition to the Macedonian king, Philip II, the father of Alexander the Great, who was rapidly expanding Macedonian territory in northern Greece and threatening Athenian allies. Demosthenes urged his fellow citizens to take active measures against Philip, while other Athenians were more conciliatory. Demosthenes' most famous opponent in Athens was Aeschines,and these two figures opposed each other in court on two famous occasions, in 343 and 330. All four speeches survive (it is very rare for speeches on both sides of a court case to survive) and the speech Demosthenes delivered in 330, known as *On the Crown*, is his masterpiece. In this oration Demosthenes defends his entire career and his continued opposition to Philip. This policy had led the Athenians into battle with Philip in 338, with a disastrous outcome for the Athenians. The defeat of the Athenians, the Thebans and the Boeotians by Philip II signaled the beginning of the end for the independent Greek city-states of the classical period. After the battle Demosthenes was chosen to deliver the state funeral oration.

Demosthenes' speech is different from all the earlier orations in this volume. First of all, we have the actual speech that Demosthenes delivered at the burial ceremony.[2] Thucydides and Plato incorporate their orations into written works of literature, and the content of the speeches are likely to be adapted to their literary contexts. Gorgias and Lysias both wrote their compositions for use in their schools, not necessarily for a real audience of Athenians and foreigners in the Ceramicus. Next,

---

[1] Plutarch, *Demosthenes* 6.3; *Lives of the ten orators* 844f.

[2] As is the case with any piece of ancient oratory, the written version may have been edited after delivery. Demosthenes refers to the speech in *On the Crown* (285). The authenticity of the speech we have as Demosthenes 60 has been contested, but there are no compelling reasons to believe it is a forgery.

this speech must come to terms with a terrible defeat.[3] It also stands apart from earlier orations in that the Athenians faced an enemy who was not Greek (many Greeks regarded the Macedonians as *barbaroi*; see glossary under **barbarian**). The catalogue of the Eponymous Heroes (27–31; see note 44 (p. 71) below) that occurs near the end of the speech is also unique. These state heroes had a collective monument in the *Agora*, the marketplace of Athens, that was a center of civic life, but this is the only corresponding passage from Athenian literature in which all ten heroes appear together and serve as a model for the Athenian citizens to emulate.

---

1   When the city decided to hold a public burial for the men buried in this grave, to honor their bravery in war,[4] and appointed me to deliver the customary speech for them, I immediately began to consider how they might obtain fitting praise. But as I started to examine the issue and think about how I might speak worthily of the dead, I realized that it was not possible. These men rejected the inborn desire for life, natural to all, and chose to die bravely rather than to live and see Greece suffer misfortune.[5] Surely the virtue which they left behind surpasses any speech.[6] I have decided to speak in the same manner as the men who have spoken here before.[7]

2   It is plain to see that this city pays serious attention to those who die in war. Among other things, we have this custom, and as part of this ceremony the city chooses a man to speak at the public burial.[8] The city knows that brave men disdain material possessions and the joy of mortal pleasures, and that instead all they desire is virtue and commendations. The city felt obliged to honor these men with speeches that would most likely meet this desire, so that the good reputation which these men 3   possessed in life may be granted to them in death too. If I saw that they only had courage out of all those qualities that constitute virtue, I would praise that and be done with the rest. But they were probably excellent because they were well born, and were strictly brought up and

---

[3] Sections 19–24 explicitly discuss that loss on the battlefield and are not paralleled in the other surviving orations.

[4] "Bravery" is *andres agathoi*; see glossary under **brave**.

[5] On this euphemism for defeat in war see glossary under **chance** and note 39 (p. 35) on Lysias.

[6] Lysias (1) and Hyperides (1–2) speak along similar lines about a speech being unable to equal the accomplishments of the dead. Thucydides (35.1) and Plato (236e) are less doubtful.

[7] For other references to previous speakers see note 10 (p. 28) on Lysias.

[8] On the appointment of the speaker see note 8 (p. 46) on Plato.

lived ambitiously.[9] I would be ashamed if I were caught leaving out any of these factors.

4   I will begin with the origin of their families.[10] All mankind has acknowledged the noble birth of these men for a very long time. These men and each of their ancestors, one and all, can trace their origin back to a father,[11] but they also have this entire fatherland as a parent, since they are acknowledged to be born of it.[12] They are the only people who live in the land from which they were born and they hand it down to the next generation. You might say that strangers who arrive at cities and come to be called citizens there are comparable to adopted children, while these men are legitimate citizens of their fatherland be-

5 cause of their birth. You also know that the fruits on which mankind lives appeared to us first. Apart from providing the greatest benefit to all men, this fact also offers an acknowledged proof that this country is the mother of our ancestors.[13] Everything that gives birth naturally provides nourishment for its offspring, and this land has done just that.

6   The familial heritage of the ancestors of these men was very rich.[14] I hesitate before bringing up their courage and their other virtues, only because I do not want my speech to become inappropriately long. It will be useful for those who are already aware of these qualities to remember them again, but it will be even more beneficial for those who did not know these men to hear of their courage. Since these qualities arouse great admiration and it is pleasant to hear of them at length,

7 let me try to summarize them. The ancestors of the present generation, their fathers and the ones whom the family members called their fathers' fathers before them, never wronged anyone, Greek or foreign.[15] Aside from all their other traits, they were completely noble and just,

8 and in their defense of us they accomplished many fine deeds.[16] In fact

---

9 "Well born" (*gegenēsthai kalōs*) doesn't have class connotations here, but instead refers to their birth as Athenian citizens. "Strictly brought up" is *pepaideusthai sōphronōs*, literally "educated in a moderate way," with discretion and good judgment. "Ambitiously" is *philotimōs*, literally "with desire for honor."

10 See note 15 (p. 13) on Thucydides for the *genos* as a topic.

11 "Origin" here is *physis*, "nature."

12 See glossary under **born of the earth**.

13 On the produce of Athens see note 25 (p. 50) on Plato.

14 Literally, "so great were the matters pertaining to their family (*genos*)." Demosthenes now makes the transition to his narrative of the accomplishments of the Athenians. Compare Lysias 3–66 and Plato 239a–246b, and see also note 18 (p. 14) on Thucydides.

15 The Greek for "foreign" is *barbaros*; see glossary under **barbarian**.

16 "Noble" (*kalos kagathos*), literally "fine and good," sometimes has class connotations, such as "gentleman" in English.

they defeated the army of the Amazons when it opposed us, so badly that they drove them beyond the Phasis.[17] And as for the army of Eumolpus,[18] and all those others, the ones whom all our western neighbors could neither withstand nor keep out, our ancestors drove them away, not just from our own territory, but from all the Greek lands. Although Heracles used to save others, when his children came to this land as suppliants, in flight from Eurystheus, our ancestors were hailed as their saviors.[19] And in addition to all these and many other noble deeds, they did not allow the rites of the dead to be violated when Creon pre-

9 vented the Seven against Thebes from being buried.[20] I will leave aside their numerous deeds that are part of the realm of myth. Instead, I refer just to these few acts in particular, since each one provides so many noble tales that those who write in meter and composers of songs and many of the prose-writers have made their deeds the subjects of their own art.[21]

Now I will speak of other achievements, in no way inferior to those earlier deeds in worth, although they have not yet been made into myth

10 or elevated to the heroic rank, because of being more recent. Twice that earlier generation, all by themselves, warded off the army advancing from all of Asia, fighting both at land and sea.[22] With their individual risks they created a public state of security throughout all of Greece.[23] I know that what I am about to say has been said before by others, but still these men must not now be deprived of their just and fitting praise. They might rightly be judged superior to those who campaigned against Troy, because that earlier generation of men from all of Greece, however excellent they were, barely captured one particular

11 part of Asia after besieging it for ten years, while these men by them-

---

[17] On the Amazons see note 15 (p. 29) on Lysias. The Phasis river ran through Colchis and drained into the Black Sea (it is the modern Rioni river in Georgia). It was considered to be a boundary between Europe and Asia.

[18] On Eumolpus see note 31 (p. 51) on Plato.

[19] For Athenian aid to the children of Heracles see note 23 (p. 31) on Lysias.

[20] On the Athenian role in the story of the Seven against Thebes see note 18 (p. 30) on Lysias. Sophocles' *Antigone* focuses on the tension between family obligations and political authority, when Creon, the king of Thebes, forbids Antigone, the sister of Polynices and Eteocles, from providing customary funeral rites to her fallen brother.

[21] On these earlier accounts see note 35 (p. 52) on Plato and note 32 (p. 18) on Thucydides.

[22] Demosthenes' account of the Persian War is much briefer than the accounts of Lysias and Plato. See note 28 (p. 33) on Lysias.

[23] See glossary under **public and private**.

selves not only warded off an army advancing from all of the Asian continent, which had subdued all others, but they also exacted vengeance for the wrongs that had been done to the others.[24] Furthermore, they prevented the Greeks themselves from becoming too greedy and they endured any danger that happened to arise.[25] Wherever justice was stationed, they assigned themselves there, until time brought us to the generation now living.

12   I do not want you to think that I have recounted these deeds of their ancestors because I don't have anything to say about each of these men. Even if I were completely incapable of finding the appropriate words, the very virtue of these men offers much that is ready at hand and easy to relate. So, now that I have mentioned the noble birth and the greatest accomplishments of their ancestors, I would like to direct my speech right away to the achievements of these men here before us. Just as they were related to their ancestors by birth, in the same way my aim is to make a joint eulogy for both of them, since I believe that the men of the past would welcome this sort of praise, and that both groups together would be especially pleased, if they were able to share each others' virtue not only through their birth but also through the praises they receive.[26]

13   I should stop for a minute, before discussing the deeds of these men, to encourage a favorable attitude toward the dead in the non-relatives who have come with us to this burial. In fact, if I had been appointed to honor the tomb with some financial expenditure or some other spectacle of equestrian or athletic contests, the more eagerly and unsparingly I had completed these duties, the more appropriately I would appear to have acted.[27] But since I have been selected to praise these men with

---

[24] Hyperides (35) makes a similar comparison between modern events and the Trojan wars, with the same emphasis on wide-ruling opponents and Athens versus the other Greeks. This comparison works particularly well for these two speeches because their opponents, the Macedonians, can be seen as powerful foreign *barbaroi*, like the Trojans, whereas earlier speeches are all from contexts in which Greeks were fighting Greeks.

[25] According to Demosthenes, the Athenians imposed just limits not only on the Persians, but also the other Greeks. See Balot 2001, 99–135 for a study of how the historian Herodotus depicts Persian and Athenian imperialism in terms of greed.

[26] The phrase "that the men of the past would welcome this sort of praise" has been rejected by many modern editors as a mistake arising from a scribal note.

[27] Wealthy Athenian citizens were required to pay for various public expenses out of their own pockets. Some of these *liturgies* paid for the cost to maintain ships, others provided means for various aspects of the festivals, such as the games Demosthenes mentions here. The most famous

a speech, I must convince my listeners to agree with me, or else, for all my eagerness, I am afraid that I might do the opposite of what I should.

14 Wealth and speed and strength and any other qualities similar to these provide their possessors with independent advantages, and those who possess these qualities prevail in contests, even without others' consent. But the persuasive power of speech depends upon the good will of the audience. If this good will exists, even if the speech is only moderately good, it brings glory and generates favor. But if it is absent, the speech gives offense to its audience, even if it excels in rhetorical flourish.

15 There are so many accomplishments that could rightly be praised that I don't know where to begin as I consider their acts.[28] All of them come to me at once and make the choice among them difficult. Even so, I will try to follow the same order in my speech as existed in their lives.

16 From the first, they were distinguished in all their schooling and they learned the appropriate subjects at each age. They were a pleasure to all those who should be pleased: their parents, friends, and relatives. And now the memory of their relatives and friends follows their tracks; it turns to them with longing every hour and it finds many reminders

17 of their excellence. When they reached manhood, they showed their fellow-citizens what they were made of, and all mankind.[29] Yes, the beginning of every virtue is intelligence, and the end is courage.[30] With the former we judge what must be done, and with the latter we achieve

18 it. They excelled greatly in both of these capacities. Whenever all the Greeks faced some shared danger, these men were the first to recognize it and they regularly summoned everyone to safety, which is proof of their selfless attitude. The other Greeks had overlooked some dangers and made light of others when it was still possible to safely ward them off. But after they submitted to necessity and agreed to do what was necessary, these men did not hold a grudge against their ignorance, which was tainted by cowardice.[31] Instead, they came forward and offered everything they had enthusiastically: their bodies, their goods, and their allies. They rose to the occasion of the struggle and they were not stingy with their lives.

19 Whenever a battle occurs, there must be winners and losers. I

---

liturgy of this type provided for the chorus of a dramatic production. For an excellent survey of this and other fourth-century political institutions see Hansen 1991 (110–112 on liturgies).

[28] The reference to the overwhelming abundance of material is a standard trope of praise. See also Hyperides 6.

[29] Literally, "they made their nature (*physis*) well known, not just to their fellow citizens, but to all mankind."

[30] See glossary under **virtue**. Thucydides also pairs bravery on the battlefield and rational thought (see note 29 (p. 17) on Thucydides).

[31] "Ignorance ... cowardice": see note 37 (p. 70) below.

would not hesitate to say that I think those who die in battle, whatever side they are on, have no share in defeat.[32] No, the dead of both sides share equally in victory. God decides how to apportion victory among the living, but everyone who remains at his post has done his part toward this end. If a mortal succumbs to fate, he has suffered this circumstance because of chance, and in his soul he is not defeated by

20 his opponents.[33] I believe that the virtue of these men, along with the folly of our opponents, is responsible for the enemy's failure to gain access to our homeland. Each of the enemy who came into battle on that occasion learned a lesson, and they were reluctant to enter another conflict with the relatives of these men, because they understood that our nature would be the same, and that they could not count on finding an equally propitious outcome again. The clearest evidence that that is the way it was is the peace that followed. One could not find a more truthful or more beautiful confirmation than the fact that the leader of the enemy, out of admiration for the virtue of the fallen, chose to be at peace with the relatives of these men who died in battle rather than risk everything a second time.[34]

21   I think that, if someone were to ask the combatants themselves whether they thought their success was due to their own virtue and the experience and daring of their commander, or to chance, which is unpredictable and harsh, not one of them would be so shameless or bold that he would take credit for what happened. When god, who rules all, has dispensed the final result according to his will, we must acquit everyone else from the charge of cowardice, because they are only human.[35] As for the general of the enemy troops excelling over those of us who were appointed to this command, no one can reasonably blame the troops on their side or ours for that.[36]

---

[32] For this sentiment compare Lysias 31 and Plato 243d.

[33] See glossary under **chance**. *Tychē* appears in the next section as "outcome." "Fate" here is the verb *heimarthai*.

[34] In fact there was wide-spread fear in Athens that Philip would invade after the battle at Chaeronea. Hyperides put forward a proposal that women and children be evacuated and that even foreigners and slaves be armed. The orator Lycurgus refers to this decree and provides a vivid picture of the panic in the city at the time (Lycurgus, *Against Leocrates* 16 and 37).

[35] "God" here (also above in 19 and below in 31 and 37) is *daimōn*, not the more typical word *theos*. The orator wishes to avoid blaming any specific god and uses a more generic term. Eight years later (330 BC), in *On the Crown*, Demosthenes connects the defeat at Chaeronea with a *daimōn* and *tychē* (and a *theos*) (192–194).

[36] Some important manuscripts omit this sentence. Many editors reject it as a scribal note explaining the next sentence.

22   If there is anyone who deserves to be blamed for these events, it is the Thebans who were appointed as commanders for this battle.[37] No one could reasonably blame the troops on their side or ours.[38] The leaders commanded a force with an unconquered spirit and an unhesitating competitive love of honor, but they did not make proper use of **23** any of these assets. As for the rest of these matters, each man may form an opinion according to his own judgment. But one thing has become clear to all mankind alike: that the freedom of all Greece was preserved in the souls of these men. Since fate took them away, none of those who remain have put up any fight. I hope my speech will not cause any jealousy,[39] but I think that someone might truly assert that the virtue of **24** these men was the soul of Greece. At the same time as each of them breathed their last breaths, the dignity of Greece was taken away. What I am about to say may seem to be excessive, but nevertheless, I must say it. It's as if someone were to remove the light of day from the world.[40] The life that remains for us would be unpleasant and difficult. In the same way, once these men have been taken away, all the former zeal of the Greeks has faded into darkness and utter disgrace.

25   These men owe their excellent character to many factors, but not least to our constitution.[41] States which are ruled by an oligarchy arouse fear in their citizens, but they do not instill shame. Whenever a war occurs, everyone heedlessly saves himself, knowing that, so long as he wins the favor of the authorities with gifts or any other form of persuasion, even if he does disgrace himself terribly, he will not be **26** much blamed in the future. Democracies have many other good and

---

[37] The Athenians were allied with the Thebans against the Macedonians, and other passages also refer to the treachery of the Theban generals (Demosthenes, *On the Crown* 300, Dinarchus, *Against Demosthenes* 74). There may also have been some scape-goating after the defeat. The Athenian general Lysicles was tried, probably on the charge of treason, and put to death (Diodorus Siculus 16.88.1).

[38] "The troops" is *hoi polloi*, literally "the masses" or "the many."

[39] Thucydides (35.2) is also concerned about the jealousy his speech may arouse.

[40] Another simile from the natural world, which some have seen as an answer to this comparison, may be found in Hyperides 5 (see note 5 (p. 79) on Hyperides). In a funeral oration delivered in 440 Pericles likened the loss of the youth of Athens to taking the Spring out of the year (the fragment is preserved at Aristotle, *Rhetoric* 1365a). On this oration see p. 5.

[41] For the topic of the constitution, see glossary under **constitution** and note 19 (p. 14) on Thucydides. The contrast between oligarchy and democracy and the emphasis on fear and shame closely echo Thucydides 37.

just aspects, to which its admirers must cling.[42] Freedom of speech, which depends upon the truth, cannot avoid revealing the truth. Those who act shamefully cannot please everyone, and as a result just one man with a genuine complaint is able to cause grief. Even those who themselves would not utter accusations enjoy hearing others making them. These men all rightly feared these sorts of charges and the shame of continued reproach, but they bravely submitted to the danger brought on by the enemy, and choose a noble death rather than a shameful life.[43]

27   That is what I have to say about the qualities these men shared that inspired them to die nobly: namely, their birth, education, good habits, and the basis of our entire constitution. I will now speak about the factors arising out of their individual Athenian tribes which inspired them to be brave.[44] All of the Erechtheidae knew that their namesake, Erechtheus, in order to save his homeland, destroyed his own daughters, who were known as the Hyacinthidae, by handing them over to a certain death.[45] As a result they believed that it would be shameful if they,

---

[42] See note 21 (p. 15) on Thucydides for other descriptions of Athenian democracy.

[43] This sentence closely echoes Thucydides 42.4. See note 36 (p. 19) on Thucydides.

[44] Each citizen was a member of one of the ten Athenian tribes, and the military and political institutions of the city were based on this system. The system was instituted by the statesman Cleisthenes at the end of the sixth century on a geographic basis. Each of these ten tribes was made up of three divisions from various parts of the greater Attica peninsula, one from the coast, one from the interior, and one from the city itself. Each of these divisions included anywhere from one to eight or nine districts (*dēmoi*). The tribes were named after various heroes selected by the oracle at Delphi. Aristotle, *Constitution of the Athenians* 21.2–6 and Herodotus 5.66 and 69 are the primary sources for Cleisthenes' reforms to the political organization of Attica. This is the only passage in Athenian literature which features such a catalogue of the eponymous heroes. Scholars have suggested that the catalogue serves here as "a mythical orchestration of the theme of victorious defeat" (Loraux 1986, 141; cf. also 127 and 389 n. 155) or a diversion to avoid the subject of the recent defeat (Kennedy 1963, 164–165). For discussion of each of these heroes in Attica see Kearns 1989.

[45] The "-dae" suffix is added to a proper name to mean "the children of." For example, "Erechtheidae" refers to the members of the tribe named after Erechtheus, who are literally "the children of Erechtheus." The Hyacinthidae, the daughters of the legendary king Erechtheus, were sacrificed during the struggle with Eumolpus (see note 31 (p. 51) on Plato). There were cults for them in Athens and they were believed to be es-

when their ancestor born of the immortals had done everything to save his country, should appear to care more for their mortal bodies than for
28 immortal glory. The Aegeidae were not unaware that Theseus, the son of Aegeus, was the first to establish political equality in the city.[46] They believed that it would be terrible to betray his policy, and they chose to die rather than to live as cowards while this freedom was destroyed among the Greeks. The Pandionidae are the inheritors of Procne and Philomela, the daughters of Pandion, who took vengeance upon Tereus for his crime against them.[47] They considered life not worth living, unless they displayed a spirit akin to their ancestors when they saw Greece
29 being assaulted.[48] The Leontidae had heard stories about the daughters of Leos and how they gave themselves to the citizens as a sacrifice for the good of their country.[49] When they had so much manly courage,[50] their descendants understood that it would not be right for them, being men, to appear to be inferior to those women. The Acamantidae used to recall the passage where Homer says that Acamas sailed to Troy to save his mother Aethra.[51] He experienced every danger in order to save his mother. How could they not submit to every danger in an effort to save

---

pecially helpful to soldiers (Euripides, fragment 65.87–89 (Austin)).

[46] Theseus, the legendary king of Athens who appears in many tragedies, is mentioned in all of the funeral orations only here. Elsewhere the orators refer to his deeds, such as the defeat of the Amazons, but these acts are attributed anonymously to the whole Athenian people, rather than a specific individual.

[47] Pandion was a mythical king of Athens. The story of his daughters is told at Apollodorus 3.14.8. Procne's husband Tereus raped Philomela and cut out her tongue. She embroidered a narrative of this act in a tapestry and Procne punished him by killing their son Itys and feeding him to his father. Tereus then learned of these acts and sought revenge, but all of them were turned into birds by the gods.

[48] "Assaulted" is the verb *hybrizesthai*, which is related to the term *hybris* and describes all sorts of violence, including rape. Hyperides uses similar language to describe Macedonian violence (20).

[49] The daughters of Leos, like the Hyacinthidae, sacrificed themselves when the Delphic oracle revealed that this act would end a plague in Athens. For discussion of this mythological motif of sacrificed maidens see Parke and Wormell 1956, 1.295–296.

[50] See glossary under **manly courage**.

[51] Aethra was the mother of Theseus and the grandmother of Acamas. She appears in the *Iliad* as a maid to Helen in Troy (3.144), but the story of her rescue appears in the Epic Cycle of poems on the aftermath of the Trojan War. The former passage was probably inserted into the *Iliad* by later Athenians, who used the story of Aethra to justify their imperial claims on the city of Amphipolis in the fifth century.

30 all of their parents at home? The Oeneidae were aware that Semele, the daughter of Cadmus, had a son who cannot be named in the presence of this grave, and that he had a son Oeneus, who was referred to as their original ancestor.[52] Since the present danger threatened both of their cities, they supposed they should put forth every effort for the sake of both. The Cecropidae knew that their founding ancestor was said by some to be a dragon, and by others to be human, for no other reason than that his intellect was similar to that of a man, while his strength was akin to that of a dragon.[53] They understood that they should act

31 in a manner worthy of both creatures. The Hippothoöntidae recalled the wedding of Alope, who gave birth to Hippothoön, and they know that he was their original ancestor.[54] In keeping with the solemnity of the occasion, I will avoid speaking too clearly about this wedding. They supposed that they ought to be seen doing deeds worthy of these ancestors. The Aeantidae knew that Aias, when he was robbed of a reward for his valor, considered life not worth living.[55] When the god gave the prize to another, they realized that they must die fighting off their enemy, so that they would not suffer anything they did not deserve. The Antiochidae did not forget that Antiochus was the son of Heracles.[56] They believed that they must either live in a manner worthy of their predecessors or else die nobly.

32   The living relatives of these dead are to be pitied,[57] because they

---

[52] See note 26 (p. 50) on Plato on this avoidance of naming the Olympians at a funeral. Dionysus was the son of Semele. There are no myths associated with Oeneus. "Both of their cities" in the following sentence refers to Athens and Thebes, where Cadmus ruled, since these were the two cities representing the Greeks at Chaeronea.

[53] Cecrops was an early ruler of Athens thought to have literally been born of the earth (see glossary under **born of the earth**). As an early leader he came to be associated with some of the first institutions of civilization, such as writing and funerary customs. He was often depicted on vase paintings as half-snake, symbolizing his origins from the Attic soil.

[54] Hippothoön was worshiped as a cult hero in Eleusis (Pausanias 1.38.4). Demosthenes avoids mentioning his parents' wedding because his father was an Olympian god, Poseidon (see note 26 (p. 50) on Plato on this taboo).

[55] After the fall of Troy, Aias (Ajax in Latin) and Odysseus competed for the arms of Achilles. Sophocles' *Aias* depicts the aftermath of the decision in Odysseus' favor. In Athens there was a cult for the son of Aias, Eurysaces, and honors for Aias may have arisen in the sixth century, when Athens had ambitions toward Salamis, Aias' homeland.

[56] There are no myths associated with Antiochus, but there's some evidence he was worshiped in Attica (Kearns 1989, 149).

[57] On this consolation see note 41 (p. 20) on Thucydides.

have lost such fine men and affectionate companions, and because our fatherland is now deserted, and full of tears and sorrow. But they are blessed, if we add it all up correctly.[58] In the first place, instead of the short period of a lifetime they are leaving behind an ageless fame that will last for a long time, for all eternity.[59] Because of their glorious reputation their children will be known and cared for and their parents will be respected and looked after in old age. Both will have fame of

33 these men as a consolation for their grief. Secondly, they will not become sick in their bodies or distressed in their souls in the same way as the living, who are afflicted by these circumstances. These men will receive the customary honors with great honor and much admiration. Only those who are buried by the whole fatherland in a public ceremony receive universal praise.[60] Their relatives and the citizens are not the only ones who miss them; the whole region we call Greece and indeed the greater part of the world share the grief. How could they not be

34 considered blessed, when it could reasonably be asserted that they are in the company of the gods down below, and they have the same position in the islands of the blessed as the brave men of the past?[61] No one has seen them there or reported back to us concerning them, but we must assume, based on their fame, that those whom the living consider to be worthy of honors on earth will obtain the same honors down below.

35 I know it is difficult to provide any relief with a speech in our present situation. But we must try to direct our minds to comforting thoughts, such as the fact that it is noble for the women who gave birth to such great men and who are themselves also born from other great men to be seen enduring hardships more decently than others, and the fact that it is noble to be like them, whatever fortune we experience.

36 This sort of behavior would be most appropriate and honorable for the dead, and it would confer much distinction on all the city and the living. It is hard for a father and a mother to lose their children and to be without their closest care-givers as they grow old.[62] But we are proud to look upon those who have won unending honors and a public monument to their virtue and who have been rewarded

37 with sacrifices and games for all eternity. It is sorrowful for children to lose their fathers. But it is wonderful for them to inherit their fathers' glory. We know that the god, to whom all mortal men must yield, is

---

[58] Literally, "with a just calculation."

[59] "Ageless fame" is a common motif: compare Thucydides 43.2, Lysias 79–81, Hyperides 42.

[60] "Universal" (*koinos*) is juxtaposed with "in a public ceremony" (*dēmosiā*) for emphasis. See glossary under **public and private**.

[61] On the islands of the blessed see note 11 (p. 47) on Plato.

[62] On care for parents and children see note 72 (p. 61) on Plato.

the cause of this sorrow, and that the voluntary decision of these men to die nobly is the cause of their honor and glory.

My aim was not to speak at length, but to tell the truth. I ask you, after you have lamented and done what is right and customary, to depart.

Introduction

Hyperides was born in Athens around 390 to a wealthy family. Like Lysias and Demosthenes, Hyperides worked as a speechwriter, beginning in the 360s. Hyperides shared Demosthenes' fear of the growth of Macedon and he opposed other Athenian politicians who were too accommodating of Macedon. In 343, the same year that Demosthenes prosecuted Aeschines for his part in an embassy to Philip, Hyperides successfully prosecuted Philocrates for helping to craft a peace treaty between Athens and Macedon that grew out of the embassy. Hyperides supported Demosthenes in the anti-Macedonian policy that eventually lead to the battle of Chaeronea in 338 (see p. 63), in which the Athenians, the Thebans and the Boeotians were defeated by Philip II of Macedon.

Despite that defeat, many Athenians continued to hope for another opportunity to face off against the Macedonians. Philip II died in 336, and his son Alexander the Great took the rule. In 335 a revolt in the Greek city of Thebes, Athens' ally at Chaeronea, was brutally put down by Alexander. Alexander died in the Summer of 323, and at last the Athenians saw an opportunity to go to war against his general, Antipater. They had been negotiating with other Greek states and had already collected a number of mercenary soldiers in the Peloponnese, under the command of the Athenian general Leosthenes. The first season of the so-called Lamian War, in 323/322, was largely successful for the Greek forces (for a narrative see Hyperides 11–18), but the general Leosthenes, a friend of Hyperides, was killed in a minor engagement. This speech was given in a spirit of optimism at the end of that first season of war, in Spring 322. The Greek success was short-lived, and a few months later the Greeks lost the war and their independence. Both Hyperides and Demosthenes were exiled from Athens under Macedonian pressure and soon after apprehended and killed.

Like the speech of Demosthenes, Hyperides' funeral oration was also actually delivered at a burial ceremony in the form that we now have.[1] The oration provides an unusual amount of specific historic detail and discusses the general Leosthenes at length. Other orations never identify their subjects by name, let alone focus so exclusively on one individual. Like the speech of Thucydides, this oration dispenses with a traditional narrative of Athenian accomplishments (see note 11 (p. 80) below). The traditional narrative of Athenian triumphs during

---

[1] Hyperides' delivery of the funeral oration is referred to by Diodorus Siculus (18.13.5), Pseudo-Plutarch (*Lives of the Ten Orators*, 849f), and Longinus (*On the Sublime* 34.2).

the Persian Wars (see note 28 (p. 33) on Lysias) is replaced by a characterization of the Macedonians as their modern-day successors. The final description of Leosthenes in the underworld is also striking and unparalleled in the other funeral orations (see note 35 (p. 85) below).

This speech survives on a single papyrus role from antiquity, which, although it is in fairly good condition, is damaged in places (especially sections 31–34). This translation strives to render the preserved text as accurately as possible.[2] Words which are missing a few letters, but which are reasonably certain, are printed in italics in the translation. More doubtful restorations are marked off in square brackets. Editors have made these suggestions on the basis of context and comparison with other speeches. These restorations in brackets have little or no real manuscript authority and the reader must regard them with caution. In other cases there is an omission in the papyrus and no convincing restorations have been suggested. These unrestored lacunae are indicated by a pair of dashes within brackets. Information about the precise length of these lacunae is not given here, but none of these omissions is much longer than twenty characters, or just a few Greek words. We probably have almost the entire speech: fragment 1 appears to begin very close to the original beginning of the speech; and fragment 3 fills in most, if not all, of the traditional consolatory section (*paramythia*); judging from the end of the other speeches, we may be missing a sentence or two from the original speech after fragment 3.

Fragment 1

1 [– –] the words about to be spoken [over] this grave [about] Leosthenes the general and about the others who have died with him in this war. Time is a witness to the fact that they were noble men.[3] Time, which [– –] the *deeds* [– –] men, [– –] has never seen *more noble* [– – not in] all eternity [– –] has there been [either better] men than those who

2 have died or more magnificent *deeds*. [For this reason] too especially, I [am now anxious] that my speech may not live up to their accomplishments.[4] But *my confidence is* restored by the fact that you, the audience, will supply whatever details I omit. For I do not address just any audience, no, I speak before men who are themselves witnesses to

3 the deeds of those men. Our city deserves to be praised because of its

---

[2] Some of the notation of the *Translated Documents of Greece & Rome* series, which is explained at Fornara 1983, 20–21, has been adapted.

[3] The first reference to the "words" may be part of a lost beginning, or it may be taken with "witness" ("time is a witness for the words ..."). On the phrase "noble men" (*andres agathoi*) see glossary under **brave**.

[4] See note 6 (p. 64) on Demosthenes for parallels.

policy. It decided upon acts similar to those done by it before, but even more honorable and noble! We must also praise the war-time courage of the dead. They did not dishonor the virtues of their ancestors! The general Leosthenes deserves to be praised on both counts: he initiated the policy for the city and he was appointed leader of the expedition for the citizens.

4   As for the city, there is not enough time now to survey individually its earlier [accomplishments throughout] all Greece nor does this occasion call for a long speech. Nor is it easy for one man alone to narrate and call to mind deeds so numerous and so great. But I will not shrink

5 from speaking about the city summarily.[5] Just as the sun goes over all the world, separating out the seasons *appropriately* and establishing [all] the right conditions, supplying reasonable and *temperate humans* with creation and [nourishment] and [fruits] and *everything* else useful for life, in the same way too our city continuously punishes the wicked, [gives aid] to the just, [dispenses] fairness instead of *injustice* to all, and *provides* [universal safety] to the Greeks at its own [risk] and expense.

6   As for the public [deeds of the] *city* as [I said, I will refrain from detailing them]. Instead I will focus my speech on *Leosthenes* and the [others. Now] where should I begin [my speech]; what should I bring up first?[6] Should I discuss in detail the ancestry of each of them? No,

7 I suppose that is foolish.[7] If I were praising some other humans, who came from many places to settle one city, each contributing a different heritage to the mix, then I would need to trace the background of each, man by man. But since I am speaking about Athenian men, who, thanks to their common origin in their birth from the land itself,[8] have insurpassable nobility, I believe that praising the ancestors individually

---

[5] In the elaborate simile that follows Hyperides alludes to many of the motifs of traditional praises of Athens. Some brief similes can be found in earlier speeches (see note 40 (p. 70) on Demosthenes), but nothing of this scale. In just a few lines the speaker invokes Athenian pride in local produce (note 25 (p. 50) on Plato), then recalls myths of Athens defeating external invaders (see note 15 (p. 29) on Lysias and note 31 (p. 51) on Plato) and protecting foreign suppliants (see note 23 (p. 31) on Lysias), and finally calls to mind the image of Athens as the sole savior of Greece (compare Lysias 20 and Plato 245c-d). This sentence dispenses with traditional praise for glorious deeds of the past and clears the way for a detailed account of very recent events.

[6] On this rhetorical techniques see note 28 (p. 68) on Demosthenes.

[7] Next, Hyperides uses the rhetorical technique of *praeteritio*, by which a speaker draws attention to a topic by pretending to pass over it, to highlight the *genos* of the dead. For the topic see note 15 (p. 13) on Thucydides.

[8] See glossary under **born of the earth**.

8 is *excessive*. Now I should mention their education, and how they were *raised* and *educated* in great *moderation* when they were children, as [– –] are accustomed to [– –]. But I suppose [everyone] knows that we educate our children [for this reason], so that they may *become* brave.[9] Since these men were distinguished in *virtue* at war, it is obvious that 9 they were taught well as children.[10] I think it is simplest to discuss their virtue in war, and how they were responsible for many benefits to their fatherland and to the other Greeks.

10 I will begin first with the general, as is right.[11] Leosthenes saw all of Greece humbled and [– –] cowering, destroyed by those working against their own fatherland and accepting bribes from Philip and Alexander.[12] When he saw that our city *needed* a man, and all Greece [needed] a city that *could* lead them to freedom, he offered himself to his *native* 11 *city*, and his city to the Greeks. After he composed a mercenary force and was appointed general of the city's force,[13] he defeated the first opponents to the freedom of the Greeks, the Boeotians, Macedonians, 12 and Euboeans and their other allies, in Boeotia.[14] From there he went

---

[9] See glossary under **brave**.

[10] See glossary under **virtue**. Loraux 1986, 109–110 sees this passage as a reply to the conception of *aretē* put forward by Demosthenes (17). She perhaps over-emphasizes the connection made by Demosthenes between education, or *paideia*, and *aretē*, and then sees this passage as a return to a more traditional definition of *aretē* as military valor.

[11] Hyperides avoids the typical narrative of Athenian accomplishments (like Pericles, see note 18 (p. 14) on Thucydides) and instead focuses on the most recent campaign season. He provides much more historical detail about the recent past than other orations do, and is the only orator who focuses on an individual victim of the war at all. The general of the Lamian War is perhaps the same as Leosthenes son of Leosthenes from the deme of Cephale who is mentioned on a few inscriptions from the early 320s as a general and sponsor of a naval ship. He died in the winter of 323/322 when hit by a stone during the siege of Lamia (see note 16 (p. 81) below).

[12] Allegations of bribery were common for ambassadors from Athens to Macedon. In a famous trial Hyperides had already successfully prosecuted Philocrates on such a charge in 343.

[13] Many Greek mercenaries who had been exiled to serve under Alexander in Asia were freed to return to Greece at the beginning of 324. Leosthenes, with authorization from the Athenian council, ferried troops to the southern Peloponnese, where they waited for Alexander's death (Diodorus Siculus 17.111.1–3). On the presence of foreigners at the ceremony and perhaps also among the fallen being buried see note 60 (p. 41) on Lysias.

[14] After Alexander died in the summer of 323 the Athenians went to war.

to Thermopylae and occupied the pass, through which the barbarians
had previously marched against the Greeks. He denied Antipater entry
into Greece,[15] and after the confrontation and victory there, he shut
13 Antipater in at Lamia and laid siege to the place.[16] He enlisted the
Thessalians, the Phocians and the Aetolians and all the others nearby
as allies, and they, whom Philip and Alexander were proud of ruling
against their will, willingly gave Leosthenes the command.[17] Although
he was able to master any situation he chose, he could not prevail over
14 fate. It is right to thank Leosthenes not only for what he did *at first*
[– –], but also for the battle *which occurred* later after *his* death, and
for the [– –] goods that came out of this campaign for the Greeks.[18]
Today we build our future achievement on the foundations laid down
by Leosthenes.

15   Please don't think that I am not making a speech for the other
citizens, [– –] that I eulogize Leosthenes alone.[19] My praise of Leosthenes [in] these battles, is also a eulogy for the others citizens. For just
as good planning depends on the general, so victory in the field comes
from those willing to risk their lives. *As a result*, whenever I praise
the victorious outcome, along with the leadership of Leosthenes I also
16 eulogize the virtue of the others. Who would not justly praise the citizens who died in the war and gave up their lives for the freedom of the
Greeks? They believed that the clearest proof of their *willingness* to
17 provide freedom to Greece was dying for her in battle. The occurrence

---

In addition to his mercenaries, Leosthenes also received support from
the Aetolians and others. These forces quickly defeated the Boeotians,
the main supporters of the Macedonians in the region (Diodorus Siculus
18.9–11).

[15] The Greeks defeated the Macedonian general Antipater at Thermopylae, and he then took refuge to the north at Lamia to await support
(Diodorus Siculus 18.12.4). On the battle of Thermopylae in 480 see
note 36 (p. 35) on Lysias. See also glossary under **barbarian**.

[16] The siege at Lamia dragged on unsuccessfully and eventually the general was killed in a minor engagement (Diodorus Siculus 18.13).

[17] This sentence is in the wrong place in the narrative. These alliances
were arranged prior to Alexander's death (Diodorus Siculus 17.111.3
and 18.9.5).

[18] In early 322 the Greeks abandoned the siege at Lamia and had a minor
victory over Macedonian forces coming to aid those at Lamia (Diodorus
Siculus 18.15.1–4,). This temporary success was overturned by significant defeats at Abydus and Crannon later that year.

[19] In the following passage Hyperides uses two overlapping terms: "praise"
(*epainos*) and "eulogy" (*egkōmion*). In general, the former term is more
widely used and has a wider semantic range, while the latter often refers
to specific types of poems or speeches.

of the *earlier* battle in Boeotia contributed greatly to their eagerness to fight for *Greece*. For they saw the city of Thebes pitiably obliterated from the face of the earth, its acropolis garrisoned by the Macedonians, the bodies of the inhabitants enslaved and foreigners parceling out the land.[20] As a result, the presence of these terrible sights before their eyes provided them with the unwavering courage to risk their lives readily.

18   The battle for Thermopylae and Lamia proved to be no less glorious for them than that which they fought in Boeotia, not only because they defeated Antipater and his allies, but also because of the location where the battle occurred. All the Greeks who arrive at the Amphictyonic meeting twice a year will be witness to the accomplishments of these men.[21] As they assemble at that place they will recall the virtue

19   of these men. None of those who came before ever fought for more noble goals or against stronger adversaries, or with fewer allies. They believed that their own virtue was strength, and that their courage, even without a great number of bodies, was a numerical advantage. They made freedom something common for everyone, but they bestowed the glory that came from their deeds as a private crown just for their fatherland.[22]

20   We should also consider what we think would have happened if they had not fought in their manner. Would the whole world not be subject to one master and would Greece not be forced to treat his temper as law? In short, the insolence of Macedon, and not the power of justice, would prevail everywhere. As a result, the abuses of each and every

21   woman, maiden, and even every child, would be unceasing.[23] That *is* clear from what we are compelled [to do] even now: to look upon sacrifices for mortals, to see the statues, the altars, and the temples of the gods neglected, while those for men are carefully celebrated, and to be

22   forced to honor their slaves as cult heroes.[24] When the rites owed to

---

[20] Alexander razed the city of Thebes in 335 after it tried to revolt, with much support from the Athenians and Demosthenes in particular, from his rule (see Plutarch, *Alexander* 11–12).

[21] The Delphic Amphictyony was a political and religious alliance of central Greek states, probably founded originally to control access to the pass at Thermopylae.

[22] See glossary under **public and private**.

[23] Compare Lysias 36 for similar worry about offenses against one's family by the victorious enemy. Hyperides later (36) will again praise the dead for protecting Athenian women. "Abuses" is the plural of *hybris*, which can refer to many sorts of violent acts, including rape; see also note 48 (p. 72) on Demosthenes. The translation here follows the text of the papyrus, but some editors suspect a problem with the text.

[24] Philip came to be associated with Zeus and may have received cult honors. There was also a debate in Athens on the question of granting Alexander similar honors. The reference to their slaves refers to

the gods are abrogated on account of the boldness of the Macedonians, what must we suppose would happen to the social customs owed to humans? Would they not be completely destroyed? The more frightening we judge these premonitions, the more praise we must believe the dead

23 to have earned. On no campaign was the soldiers' virtue more apparent than on this one, when they had to go into battle everyday and fight more battles in one season than the blows which all others had suffered before. They had to endure severe weather and such great shortages of daily necessities with so much self-control that it is difficult to relate in words.[25]

24 Considering that Leosthenes persuaded the citizens to endure so many hardships without hesitation, and to offer themselves eagerly as fellow fighters alongside such a great general, surely we must believe them fortunate because of the excellence they displayed, and not unlucky because of their loss of life.[26] These men acquired immortal glory for the price of a mortal body and they also secured public freedom

25 for the Greeks with their own individual virtue.[27] [Nothing] provides complete happiness in the absence of independence. The voice of law, not a man's threat, must have authority over people, if they are to be happy.[28] An accusation shouldn't cause fear among free men, only proof. The safety of the citizens shouldn't depend upon those who flatter their masters and slander their fellow citizens, but rather upon faith

26 in the law. For all these reasons they performed labor after labor. With their daily risks they lessened the fear of the citizens and the Greeks for all time. They gave up their lives so that others could live well.

27 Because of them their fathers have become famous and their mothers are admired among the citizens. Their sisters have rightly entered into suitable weddings and will continue to do so. The children of these men who have died — no, it is not right to use that term for men who lost their lives fighting on behalf of such a noble cause — rather, of men who have exchanged life for an eternal post, will have their virtue as an

28 introduction to the good will of the people.[29] If death, which is most

---

Alexander's closest companion Hephaestion, whose worship Alexander advocated after he died in 324. For the evidence and more discussion of these early instances of Greek ruler worship, see Badian 1981.

[25] The hardships of battle were a standard theme in Attic literature. Compare Aeschylus, *Agamemnon* 559–566 on the Greeks at Troy and Plato, *Symposium* 219e–220b on Socrates at Potidaea.

[26] See glossary under **chance**.

[27] See glossary under **public and private**.

[28] On Athenian attitudes toward the law see note 22 (p. 15) on Thucydides.

[29] See note 69 (p. 60) on Plato for a similar doubt about the misfortune of the dead.

grievous for others, has brought them great advantages, how can we not judge them fortunate, and how can we say that they have lost their lives, instead of saying that a new birth has occurred for them, more excellent than their first? Then they were senseless children, but now

29 they have become brave men.[30] And then they displayed their virtue over a long period of time and amid many perils. Now as a result of this [– –] become known to everyone and remembered for their courage.[31]

30   On what occasion will we not recall the virtue of these men?[32] In what place will we not see them as the object of pride and esteemed praise? Will they not come to mind if the city does well? Will we praise and remember any others for what came about because of these men? Perhaps they won't be remembered by those who are individually prosperous? But we safely enjoy those successes thanks to the virtue of

31 these men. In the eyes of what generation will they not be blessed?[33] [– –] among the [– –] *fearless* [– –] life [– –] to have become [– –] because of *them*? [– – among] their peers? [– –] death [– –] nobly [– –] by *far*

32 [– –] has [– – among the] youth [– –] not the [– –] *are eager* [– –] exam-

33 ple [– –] the virtue [– –] for everyone, not [– –] to [– –] *them* [– –] not. Who [– –] Greek [– –] of the things [– –] among [– –] of the Phrygians[34] [– –] *campaign* [– –] but of the [– –] most [– –] to all [– –] *songs to praise*

34 [– –] for more [– –] about Leosthenes [– –] and of those [– –] in war [– –] for the sake of pleasure [– –] the things endured [– –] what *would be* sweeter for *the Greeks* [than – –] of those [– –] freedom [– –]? If such a [– –] was [motivated by profit], what speech would confer more advantage on the souls of those who will hear it than one which eulogizes

35 virtue and brave men? All this makes it clear that we and everyone else

---

[30] See glossary under **brave**.

[31] The text of the papyrus is faulty in this sentence. Something appears to have fallen out.

[32] Lysias (74) asks a series of similar questions. The questions are rhetorical: the orator emphasizes that the dead will always be celebrated everywhere.

[33] At this point more than half of a column of text is missing from the papyrus. The details of the text cannot be recovered with any certainty. Hyperides probably continues listing the benefits the fallen have given to the Athenians, who are divided into age-groups. First he refers to the elder citizens and the secure life they will enjoy. Then he turns to the soldiers' peers, who can live without fear, and the young Athenians, who will benefit from the good example set by the dead. Next the orator may refer to the praise the soldiers will receive in speeches and songs, and compare the songs sung of the Trojan War. Finally this section emphasizes how pleasant it will be to recall the valor of the fallen.

[34] Phrygia was a region of Anatolia in Asia Minor. Hyperides must be making a comparison with the Trojan War.

must honor them.

We should consider who will welcome their leader in Hades.[35] Don't you think we would see some [demi-gods], as we call them, the ones who fought in the struggle against *Troy*, welcoming and admiring Leosthenes?[36] His deeds were of the same nature, but he surpassed them, since they, with the help of all Greece, captured only one city, while he, with the help of his native city alone, brought down the entire

36 ruling power of Europe and Asia. They came to the defense of one women who had been violated, but he, together with these men now being buried with him, prevented the violence that threatened all the

37 women of Greece.[37] Let's also consider the accomplishments of those who lived later, which matched their ancestors' virtue. I am referring to the men who fought with Miltiades and Themistocles and the rest, the ones who brought honor to their native city by freeing Greece, and

38 who made their own lives glorious.[38] Leosthenes greatly excelled them in courage and wits, because they warded off the barbarian force when it was already entering Greece, while he did not allow them even to enter. Furthermore, they saw the enemy fighting on the Greek home front, but he prevailed over his adversaries on their own ground.[39]

39   I think that those two who showed their mutual friendship most firmly to the people, I mean Harmodius and Aristogiton, consider *nobody to be more closely related to them than* Leosthenes and his fellow combatants.[40] There are not any others with whom they would pre-

---

[35] See note 11 (p. 47) on Plato for other formulations of the afterlife. This detailed picture of Leosthenes meeting earlier generals and patriots in the underworld is unparalleled in other funeral orations. But Socrates, in his defense speech, similarly looks forward to meeting great men of the past in Hades (Plato, *Apology* 41a–c).

[36] On the comparison of recent events and the Trojan War see note 24 (p. 67) on Demosthenes.

[37] On this theme, see note 23 (p. 82) above and note 48 (p. 72) on Demosthenes.

[38] Miltiades was the Athenian general at Marathon (see note 29 (p. 33) on Lysias), Themistocles at Salamis (see note 40 (p. 36) on Lysias). Whereas other orations describe the triumphs of the Persian Wars as a model for the fallen to strive to live up to, let alone surpass, Hyperides skipped over any narrative of those events and now boldly asserts that the men he praises are superior to those at that time.

[39] Thucydides also singles out this point (39.2).

[40] Harmodius and Aristogiton were celebrated in Athens for their efforts to rid the city of the Pisistratus and his sons, tyrannical rulers during the sixth century (see Thucydides 6.53–59). They are not mentioned in other funeral orations, but here the comparison reinforces the characterization of the Macedonians as tyrants.

fer to associate in Hades. Rightly so, since Leosthenes and his men achieved no less than those two. In fact, if it must be said, these men attained even greater achievements. Those two destroyed the tyrants of their native city, but these men destroyed the tyrants of all Greece.

40 How noble and unbelievable was the bravery exercised by these men, how glorious and magnificent was the choice which they made, how excellent was their virtue and courage in danger, which they offered for the common freedom of the Greeks [– –]

Fragment 2

[– –] other [– –] many [– –]

Fragment 3

41 Perhaps it is difficult to console those who are so bereaved.[41] Your sufferings are not eased by a speech or by law. Instead your individual nature and your love for the deceased imposes a limit on your grief. Even so, you must be courageous and control your grief as much as you can, and think not only of their death, but also of the virtue which

42 they have left behind. Although they have suffered a mournful fate, they have also done deeds worthy of great praise. Although they did not live to see old age, they have gained ageless glory and have become blessed in every respect.[42] For those of them who died without children, the praise of the Greeks will serve as immortal offspring. As for those who left behind children, the good will of their native city will act as

43 a guardian for them.[43] In addition to these things, if death is similar to not existing, then they are spared from sicknesses and suffering and the other things which trouble mortal lives. If there is consciousness in Hades and the dead enjoy the care of the divine, as we believe, then those who defended the honors of the gods when they were under attack will receive the utmost attention and care from the divinity.

Uncertain Fragment 1

ageless time

---

[41] On the consolation see note 41 (p. 20) on Thucydides.

[42] "Ageless glory" echoes earlier expressions: compare Thucydides 43.2, Lysias 79–81, and Demosthenes 32.

[43] On public support of the children see note 72 (p. 61) on Plato.

Introduction

Although this volume focuses on funeral orations from classical Athens, some readers may appreciate convenient access to the texts of these speeches delivered during the American Civil War. These speeches were given on November 19, 1863 at the dedication ceremony for a military cemetery in Gettysburg, Pennsylvania to commemorate the fallen soldiers at the battle that occurred at that location more than four months earlier, from July 1 to July 3. That battle is often seen as a turning point in the Civil War, but fighting continued for more than a year, until the surrender of the confederate forces in April 1865.

The American Civil War did not involve a foreign adversary. The speeches of Thucydides, Lysias and Plato were all delivered in similar circumstances, when the Athenians were at war with other Greeks. And both of the principal speakers, President Abraham Lincoln and Senator Edward Everett, formerly a professor of Greek at Harvard, probably had these classical examples of the genre in mind (the Hyperides papyrus had only come to light five years before). Some of the frequent echoes are noted here.

Lincoln's speech was remarkably short, and is here presented in its entirety. Like the ancients, Lincoln contrasts the sacrifice of the dead with the obligations owed by the living. He refers to the fallen men generically, as do all the Athenian orations except that of Hyperides. The Everett speech, in contrast to Lincoln's, is very long and can only be excerpted here. The paragraph numbers are those of Wills 1992, 213–247, a recent study of the addresses at Gettysburg and their classical models. Tritle 2000, 143–164 also compares Lincoln's speech with its Greek models.

Lincoln

Four score and seven years ago our fathers brought forth on this continent a new nation, conceived in liberty and dedicated to the proposition that all men are created equal.

Now we are engaged in a great civil war, testing whether that nation or any nation so conceived and so dedicated can long endure. We are met on a great battlefield of that war. We have come to dedicate a portion of that field as a final resting-place for those who here gave their lives that that nation might live.[1] It is altogether fitting and proper that we should do this.

---

[1] The themes of sacrifice for the country and eternal praise for the dead (next paragraph) echo Thucydides 43.2.

But in a larger sense, we cannot dedicate, we cannot consecrate, we cannot hallow this ground. The brave men, living and dead who struggled here have consecrated it far above our poor power to add or detract. The world will little note nor long remember what we say here, but it can never forget what they did here.[2] It is for us the living rather to be dedicated here to the unfinished work which they who fought here have thus far so nobly advanced. It is rather for us to be here dedicated to the great task remaining before us — that from these honored dead we take increased devotion to that cause for which they gave the last full measure of devotion — that we here highly resolve that these dead shall not have died in vain, that this nation under God shall have a new birth of freedom, and that government of the people, by the people, for the people shall not perish from the earth.

Everett

1   Standing beneath this serene sky, overlooking these broad fields now reposing from the labors of the waning year, the mighty Alleghanies dimly towering before us, the graves of our brethren beneath our feet, it is with hesitation that I raise my poor voice to break the eloquent silence of God and Nature. But the duty to which you have called me must be performed; — grant me, I pray you, your indulgence and your sympathy.[3]

2   It was appointed by law in Athens, that the obsequies of the citizens who fell in battle should be performed at the public expense, and in the most honorable manner.[4] Their bones were carefully gathered up from the funeral pyre where their bodies were consumed, and brought home to the city. There, for three days before the interment, they lay in state, beneath tents of honor, to receive the votive offerings of friends and relatives, — flowers, weapons, precious ornaments, painted vases (wonders of art, which after two thousand years adorn the museums of modern Europe), — the last tributes of surviving affection. Ten coffins of funereal cypress received the honorable deposit, one for each of the tribes of the city, and an eleventh in memory of the unrecognized, but not therefore unhonored, dead, and of those whose remains could not be recovered. On the fourth day the mournful procession was formed: mothers, wives, sisters, daughters, led the way, and to them it was permitted by the simplicity of ancient manners to utter aloud their lamentations for the beloved and the lost; the male relatives and friends of the deceased

---

[2] See glossary under **brave**; compare also note 59 (p. 74) on Demosthenes.

[3] Everett's hesitation is reminiscent of the classical orators' worry about living up to the task at hand. See note 6 (p. 64) on Demosthenes.

[4] The description of the Athenian tradition in this paragraph draws heavily on Thucydides 34.

followed; citizens and strangers closed the train. Thus marshaled, they moved to the place of interment in that famous Ceramicus, the most beautiful suburb of Athens, which had been adorned by Cimon, the son of Miltiades,[5] with walks and fountains and columns, — whose groves were filled with altars, shrines, and temples, — whose gardens were kept forever green by the streams from the neighboring hills, and shaded with the trees sacred to Minerva and coeval with the foundation of the city, — whose circuit enclosed "the olive grove of Academe, | Plato's retirement, where the Attic bird | Trilled his thick-warbled note the summer long,"[6] whose pathways gleamed with the monuments of the illustrious dead, the work of the most consummate masters that ever gave life to marble. There, beneath the overarching plane-trees, upon a lofty stage erected for the purpose, it was ordained that a funeral oration should be pronounced by some citizen of Athens, in the presence of the assembled multitude.

3   Such were the tokens of respect required to be paid at Athens to the memory of those who had fallen in the cause of their country. For those alone who fell at Marathon a peculiar honor was reserved.[7] As the battle fought upon that immortal field was distinguished from all others in Grecian history for its influence over the fortunes of Hellas, — as it depended upon the event of that day whether Greece should live, a glory and a light to all coming time, or should expire, like the meteor of a moment; so the honors awarded to its martyr-heroes were such as were bestowed by Athens on no other occasion. They alone of all her sons were entombed upon the spot which they had forever rendered famous. Their names were inscribed upon ten pillars erected upon the monumental tumulus which covered their ashes (where, after six hundred years, they were read by the traveler Pausanias),[8] and although the columns, beneath the hand of time and barbaric violence, have long since disappeared, the venerable mound still marks the spot where they fought and fell, — "That battle-field where Persia's victim-horde | First bowed beneath the brunt of Hellas' sword."[9]

4   And shall I, fellow-citizens, who, after an interval of twenty-three centuries, a youthful pilgrim from the world unknown to ancient Greece,

---

[5] On Miltiades see note 38 (p. 85) on Hyperides.

[6] John Milton, *Paradise Regain'd* 4.244–246.

[7] The Gettysburg speeches differed from the Athenian funeral orations in that it was delivered on the site of the battle. Everett refers to the burial of the dead at Marathon as a parallel, drawing on Thucydides 34.5. On the battle of Marathon see note 29 (p. 33) on Lysias.

[8] Pausanias describes the monument at Marathon in his *Description of Greece* 1.32.3.

[9] Lord Byron, *Childe Harold's Pilgrimage*, canto 2, stanza 89.

have wandered over that illustrious plain,[10] ready to put off the shoes from off my feet, as one that stands on holy ground, — who have gazed with respectful emotion on the mound which still protects the dust of those who rolled back the tide of Persian invasion, and rescued the land of popular liberty, of letters, and of arts, from the ruthless foe, — stand unmoved over the graves of our dear brethren, who so lately, on three of those all-important days which decide a nation's history, — days on whose issue it depended whether this august republican Union, founded by some of the wisest statesmen that ever lived, cemented with the blood of some of the purest patriots that ever died, should perish or endure, — rolled back the tide of an invasion, not less unprovoked, not less ruthless, than that which came to plant the dark banner of Asiatic despotism and slavery on the free soil of Greece? Heaven forbid! And could I prove so insensible to every prompting of patriotic duty and affection, not only would you, fellow-citizens, gathered many of you from distant States, who have come to take part in these pious offices of gratitude, — you, respected fathers, brethren, matrons, sisters, who surround me, — cry out for shame, but the forms of brave and patriotic men who fill these honored graves would heave with indignation beneath the sod.

5   We have assembled, friends, fellow-citizens, at the invitation of the Executive of the great central State of Pennsylvania, seconded by the Governors of seventeen other loyal States of the Union, to pay the last tribute of respect to the brave men who, in the hard-fought battles of the first, second, and third days of July last, laid down their lives for the country on these hillsides and the plains before us, and whose remains have been gathered into the cemetery which we consecrate this day. As my eye ranges over the fields whose sods were so lately moistened by the blood of gallant and loyal men, I feel, as never before, how truly it was said of old that it is sweet and becoming to die for one's country.[11] I feel, as never before, how justly, from the dawn of history to the present time, men have paid the homage of their gratitude and admiration to the memory of those who nobly sacrifice their lives, that their fellow-men may live in safety and in honor. And if this tribute were ever due, to whom could it be more justly paid than to those whose last resting-place we this day commend to the blessing of Heaven and of men?

6   For consider, my friends, what would have been the consequences to the country, to yourselves, and to all you hold dear, if those who sleep beneath our feet, and their gallant comrades who survive to serve their country on other fields of danger, had failed in their duty on those

---

[10] Everett refers to the plain at Marathon, which has a burial mound for the soldiers who died there.

[11] Everett quotes a famous saying of the Roman poet Horace (*Odes* 3.2.13).

memorable days.[12] Consider what, at this moment, would be the condition of the United States, if that noble Army of the Potomac, instead of gallantly and for the second time beating back the tide of invasion from Maryland and Pennsylvania, had been itself driven from these well-contested heights, thrown back in confusion on Baltimore, or trampled down, discomfited, scattered to the four winds. What, in that sad event, would not have been the fate of the Monumental City, of Harrisburg, of Philadelphia, of Washington, the Capital of the Union, each and every one of which would have lain at the mercy of the enemy, accordingly as it might have pleased him, spurred by passion, flushed with victory, and confident of continued success, to direct his course?

23   And now the momentous day, a day to be forever remembered in the annals of the country, arrived. Early in the morning on the 1st of July the conflict began. I need not say that it would be impossible for me to comprise, within the limits of the hour, such a narrative as would do anything like full justice to the all-important events of these three great days, or to the merit of the brave officers and men of every rank, of every arm of the service, and of every loyal State, who bore their part in the tremendous struggle, — alike those who nobly sacrificed their lives for their country, and those who survive, many of them scarred with honorable wounds, the objects of our admiration and gratitude.[13] The astonishingly minute, accurate, and graphic accounts contained in the journals of the day, prepared from personal observation by reporters who witnessed the scenes and often shared the perils which they describe, and the highly valuable "Notes" of Professor Jacobs of the University in this place, to which I am greatly indebted, will abundantly supply the deficiency of my necessarily too condensed statement.

38   I must leave to others, who can do it from personal observation, to describe the mournful spectacle presented by these hillsides and plains at the close of the terrible conflict. It was a saying of the Duke of Wellington, that next to a defeat, the saddest thing is a victory. The horrors of the battle-field, after the contest is over, the sights and sounds of woe, — let me throw a pall over the scene, which no words can adequately depict to those who have not witnessed it on which no one who has witnessed it, and who has a heart in his bosom, can bear to dwell. One drop of balm alone, one drop of heavenly life-giving balm, mingles in this bitter cup of misery. Scarcely has the cannon ceased to roar, when the brethren and sisters of Christian benevolence, ministers of compassion, angels of pity, hasten to the field and the hospital, to moisten the parched tongue, to bind the ghastly wounds, to soothe the

---

[12] Hyperides (20) similarly asks his listeners to consider what would happen if the Macedonians were successful.

[13] On this theme see note 6 (p. 64) on Demosthenes.

parting agonies alike of friend and foe, and to catch the last whispered messages of love from dying lips. "Carry this miniature back to my dear wife, but do not take it from my bosom till I am gone." "Tell my little sister not to grieve for me; I am willing to die for my country." "O that my mother were here!" When since Aaron stood between the living and the dead was there ever so gracious a ministry as this? It has been said that it is characteristic of Americans to treat women with a deference not paid to them in any other country.[14] I will not undertake to say whether this is so; but I will say, that, since this terrible war has been waged, the women of the loyal States, if never before, have entitled themselves to our highest admiration and gratitude, — alike those who at home, often with fingers unused to the toil, often bowed beneath their own domestic cares, have performed an amount of daily labor not exceeded by those who work for their daily bread, and those who, in the hospital and the tents of the Sanitary and Christian Commissions, have rendered services which millions could not buy. Happily, the labor and the service are their own reward. Thousands of matrons and thousands of maidens have experienced a delight in these homely toils and services, compared with which the pleasures of the ball-room and the opera-house are tame and unsatisfactory. This on earth is reward enough, but a richer is in store for them. Yes, brothers, sisters of charity, while you bind up the wounds of the poor sufferers, — the humblest, perhaps, that have shed their blood for the country, — forget not who it is that will hereafter say to you, "Inasmuch as ye have done it unto one of the least of these my brethren, ye have done it unto me."[15]

49   No man can deplore more than I do the miseries of every kind unavoidably incident to war. Who could stand on this spot and call to mind the scenes of the first days of July with any other feeling? A sad foreboding of what would ensue, if war should break out between North and South, has haunted me through life, and led me, perhaps too long, to tread in the path of hopeless compromise, in the fond endeavor to conciliate those who were predetermined not to be conciliated. But it is not true, as is pretended by the Rebels and their sympathizers, that the war has been carried on by the United States without entire regard to those temperaments which are enjoined by the law of nations, by our modern civilization, and by the spirit of Christianity. It would be quite easy to point out, in the recent military history of the leading European powers, acts of violence and cruelty, in the prosecution of their wars, to which no parallel can be found among us. In fact, when we consider the peculiar bitterness with which civil wars are almost invariably waged,

---

[14] Everett singles out women, as Thucydides did (45.2), but Everett has a more positive view of their contribution to the war effort.

[15] Matthew 25.40.

we may justly boast of the manner in which the United States have carried on the contest.[16] It is of course impossible to prevent the lawless acts of stragglers and deserters, or the occasional unwarrantable proceedings of subordinates on distant stations; but I do not believe there is, in all history, the record of a civil war of such gigantic dimensions where so little has been done in the spirit of vindictiveness as in this war, by the Government and commanders of the United States; and this notwithstanding the provocation given by the Rebel Government by assuming the responsibility of wretches like Quantrell, refusing quarter to colored troops, and scourging and selling into slavery free colored men from the North who fall into their hands, by covering the sea with pirates, refusing a just exchange of prisoners, while they crowd their armies with paroled prisoners not exchanged, and starving prisoners of war to death.

57   But the hour is coming and now is, when the power of the leaders of the Rebellion to delude and inflame must cease. There is no bitterness on the part of the masses. The people of the South are not going to wage an eternal war for the wretched pretexts by which this rebellion is sought to be justified. The bonds that unite us as one People,[17] — a substantial community of origin, language, belief, and law (the four great ties that hold the societies of men together); common national and political interests; a common history; a common pride in a glorious ancestry; a common interest in this great heritage of blessings; the very geographical features of the country; the mighty rivers that cross the lines of climate, and thus facilitate the interchange of natural and industrial products, while the wonder-working arm of the engineer has leveled the mountain-walls which separate the East and West, compelling your own Alleghanies, my Maryland and Pennsylvania friends, to open wide their everlasting doors to the chariot-wheels of traffic and travel, — these bonds of union are of perennial force and energy, while the causes of alienation are imaginary, factitious, and transient. The heart of the People, North and South, is for the Union. Indications, too plain to be mistaken, announce the fact, both in the East and the West of the States in rebellion. In North Carolina and Arkansas the fatal charm at length is broken. At Raleigh and Little Rock the dips of honest and brave men are unsealed, and an independent press is unlimbering its artillery. When its rifled cannon shall begin to roar, the hosts of treasonable sophistry — the mad delusions of the day — will fly like the Rebel army through the passes of yonder mountain. The weary masses of the people are yearning to see the dear old flag again floating

---

[16] Compare Plato 243e.

[17] These bonds are similar to the Athenian emphasis on their homogeneity and unique constitution. See glossary under **born of the earth** and **constitution**. Compare also note 25 (p. 50) on Plato.

upon their capitols, and they sigh for the return of the peace, prosperity, and happiness which they enjoyed under a government whose power was felt only in its blessings.

58 And now, friends, fellow-citizens of Gettysburg and Pennsylvania, and you from remoter States, let me again, as we part, invoke your benediction on these honored graves. You feel, though the occasion is mournful, that it is good to be here. You feel that it was greatly auspicious for the cause of the country, that the men of the East and the men of the West, the men of nineteen sister States, stood side by side, on the perilous ridges of the battle. You now feel it a new bond of union, that they shall lie side by side, till a clarion, louder than that which marshaled them to the combat, shall awake their slumbers. God bless the Union; — it is dearer to us for the blood of brave men which has been shed in its defense. The spots on which they stood and fell; these pleasant heights; the fertile plain beneath them; the thriving village whose streets so lately rang with the strange din of war; the fields beyond the ridge, where the noble Reynolds held the advancing foe at bay, and, while he gave up his own life, assured by his forethought and self-sacrifice the triumph of the two succeeding days; the little streams which wind through the hills, on whose banks in after-times the wondering ploughman will turn up, with the rude weapons of savage warfare, the fearful missiles of modern artillery; Seminary Ridge, the Peach-Orchard, Cemetery, Culp, and Wolf Hill, Round Top, Little Round Top, humble names, henceforward dear and famous, — no lapse of time, no distance of space, shall cause you to be forgotten. "The whole earth," said Pericles, as he stood over the remains of his fellow-citizens, who had fallen in the first year of the Peloponnesian War, — "the whole earth is the sepulcher of illustrious men."[18] All time, he might have added, is the millennium of their glory. Surely I would do no injustice to the other noble achievements of the war, which have reflected such honor on both arms of the service, and have entitled the armies and the navy of the United States, their officers and men, to the warmest thanks and the richest rewards which a grateful people can pay. But they, I am sure, will join us in saying, as we bid farewell to the dust of these martyr-heroes, that wheresoever throughout the civilized world the accounts of this great warfare are read, and down to the latest period of recorded time, in the glorious annals of our common country there will be no brighter page than that which relates the battles of Gettysburg.

---

[18] Thucydides 43.3.

Several common themes occur repeatedly throughout the various orations collected in this volume. The most important of these are listed here for reference. The references in the notes cannot list every single occurrence of these themes, and instead identify only the most significant examples.

Barbarian (*barbaros*) refers to any non-Greek speaking people (see, for example, Herodotus 1.58, and in these speeches, Gorgias 5b and Demosthenes 7), who are thought of as uncivilized because of this fact. Throughout these speeches the word *barbaros* is translated either "barbarian" or "foreign."

Born of the earth (*autochthones*) The Athenians took pride in the legend that they were born of the earth. They used this myth to account for their homogeneity and their eagerness to defend the land against foreign invaders. According to this belief, they also became civilized earlier than other races because they spent no time migrating. Rosivach 1987 and Loraux 2000 discuss this legend, which may have arisen as late as the fifth century. See Thucydides 2.36.1, Lysias 17, Plato 237c and Hyperides 7. Demosthenes (4) similarly compares the citizens of other states to adopted children.

Brave (*agathos, andres agathoi*). The phrase *andres agathoi*, literally "good men," is used frequently throughout all the funeral orations to describe the honored state achieved by the dead as a result of their courageous self-sacrifice in the field. The speeches also employ the adjective as a predicate: "to demonstrate bravery," *gignesthai agathoi*, literally "to become good," regularly describes the act of fighting and/or dying on the battlefield. The term also has class connotations ("good" = "wealthy;" compare English "well-to-do"). The funeral orations assign this almost aristocratic label to anyone who dies in battle, rich or poor. Loraux 1986, 106–108 (also see "aner agathos" in the index) discusses the scope and use of the term.

Chance (*tychē*) refers to affairs that are beyond human control. It may be rendered as "fate" or "fortune." This word is often used to soften the description of a defeat. The fallen men were beaten by *tychē*, not their opponents. Demosthenes 21 describes *tychē* as "unpredictable and harsh." See also Lysias 10. The compound *dystychia*, literally "bad chance," is used similarly, to avoid assigning specific blame for a defeat. The religious context of these speeches precludes such specificities. See also note 39 (p. 35) on Lysias.

Constitution (*politeia*) refers to more than just the formal political structure of the government. It refers to the broader political community in which a citizen participated. In Athens the people (*dēmos*) and the city were often equated. The *politeia* describes the entire public life a citizen would lead. Plato's *Republic*, which considers the nature of the ideal state, is called the *Politeia* in Greek. We also have more down-to-earth works describing various aspects of political life in Sparta and Athens (Xenophon's *Constitution of the Spartans* and the two different works, each known as the *Constitution of the Athenians*, one by the anonymous "old oligarch" and the other perhaps by Aristotle; all three are translated with notes in Moore 1975).

Danger (*kindynos*). This noun and the related verb *kindynein*, literally "to undergo a risk," frequently describe the risks the soldiers were willing to face. These terms emphasize the voluntary sacrifice the soldiers made, despite their conscious knowledge of the danger. This decision is described in detail by Thucydides (42.4) and Demosthenes (26). See also note 11 (p. 29) on Lysias.

Fairness (*epieikeia*) is the quality of tolerance or flexibility which motivated the Athenians to adapt to a particular situation or forgive and protect suppliants (see note 23 (p. 31) on Lysias). Adkins 1966, esp. 79–80 and 94–98, discusses attitudes toward this quality in fourth-century Athens, where it was treated as an important aspect of individual virtue.

Manly courage (*andreia*). This common word for "courage" derived from the word *anēr*, "man," and might literally be rendered as "manliness."

Public and private (*koinos* and *idios*). The contrast between the public (*koinos* or sometimes *dēmosiā*) benefits and the private (*idios*) risks of the soldiers is repeatedly emphasized. The danger facing Greece is repeatedly described as "shared" (*koinos*). See, for example, Thucydides 42.3, Lysias 44, Demosthenes 10 and Hyperides 24.

Speech and deeds (*logos* and *ergon/erga*) were regularly contrasted in the funeral orations and other Athenian literature of the fifth and fourth centuries. This antithesis, which is sometimes rather forced, appears very frequently in most of these funeral orations and generally in contemporary literature (for example, Thucydides 42.1–2 and 42.4, Lysias 2, Plato 244a).

Virtue (*aretē*) was an abstract quality traditionally associated with success in a competition (*agōn*). The battlefield was a key arena for demonstrating *aretē*, and in death soldiers were always considered to be successful and virtuous. For a discussion of this aspect of *aretē* see Adkins 1960, 166, 170–171. See also note 10 (p. 80) on Hyperides.

Adkins, A. W. H. (1966). "Aristotle and the Best Kind of Tragedy." *Classical Quarterly* 16: 78–102.

———. (1960). *Merit and Responsibility; A Study in Greek Values.* Oxford.

Badian, E. (1981). "The Deification of Alexander the Great." In *Ancient Macedonian Studies in honor of Charles F. Edson.* Volume 158 of *Institute for Balkan Studies.* Pages 27–71. Thessaloniki.

Balot, R. K. (2001). *Greed and Injustice in Classical Athens.* Princeton.

Burgess, T. C. (1902). *Epideictic Literature.* Chicago.

Collins, S. and Stauffer, D. (1999). *Empire and the Ends of Politics: Plato's Menexenus and Pericles' Funeral Oration.* Newburyport, Mass.

Coventry, L. (1989). "Philosophy and Rhetoric in the *Menexenus.*" *Journal of Hellenic Studies* 109: 1–15.

Fornara, C. W. (1983). *Archaic Times to the End of the Peloponnesian War.* Volume 1 of *Translated Documents of Greece & Rome.* 2d edition. Cambridge.

Goldhill, S. (1990). "The Great Dionysia and Civic Ideology." In Winkler, J. J. and Zeitlin, F. I., eds., *Nothing To Do With Dionysus? The Social Meanings of Athenian Drama.* Pages 97–129. Princeton.

Hansen, M. H. (1991). *The Athenian Democracy in the Age of Demosthenes.* Oxford.

Harding, P. (1985). *From the End of the Peloponnesian War to the Battle of Ipsus.* Volume 2 of *Translated Documents of Greece & Rome.* Cambridge.

Harris, E. M. (1992). "Pericles' Praise of Athenian Democracy. Thucydides 2.37.1." *Harvard Studies in Classical Philology* 94: 157–167.

Henry, M. (1995). *Prisoner of History: Aspasia of Miletus and her Biographical Tradition.* Oxford.

Kahn, C. H. (1963). "Plato's Funeral Oration: The Motive of the *Menexenus.*" *Classical Philology* 58: 220–234.

Kearns, E. (1989). *The Heroes of Attica.* Volume 57 of *University of London Institute of Classical Studies Bulletin supplements.* London.

Kennedy, G. A. (1963). *The Art of Persuasion in Greece.* Princeton.

Krentz, P. (1982). *The Thirty at Athens.* Ithaca.

Loraux, N. (1986). *The Invention of Athens: The Funeral Oration in the Classical City.* Cambridge, Mass. Translation of 1981 French edition by A. Sheridan.

———. (2000). *Born of the Earth: Myth and Politics in Athens.* Ithaca. Translation of 1981 French edition by S. Stewart.

MacDowell, D. M. (1982). *Gorgias. Encomium of Helen.* Bristol.

Monoson, S. S. (2000). *Plato's Democratic Entanglements: Athenian Politics and the Practice of Philosophy.* Princeton.

Moore, J. M. (1975). *Aristotle and Xenophon on Democracy and Oligarchy.* California.

Morris, I. (1992). *Death-Ritual and Social Structure in Classical Antiquity.* Key Themes in Ancient History. Cambridge.

Parke, H. W. and Wormell, D. E. W. (1956). *The Delphic Oracle.* Oxford. 2 vols.

Parker, R. (1983). *Miasma. Pollution and Purification in Early Greek Religion.* Oxford.

———. (1996). *Athenian Religion. A History.* Oxford.

Pritchett, W. K. (1985). *The Greek State at War.* Berkeley. Part 4.

Rose, M. (2000). "Fallen Heroes: Bones of Pericles' Soldiers Come to New York for Analysis." *Archaeology* no. 53/2 (March/April): 42–45.

Rosivach, V. (1987). "Autochthony and the Athenians." *Classical Quarterly* 37: 294–306.

Rusten, J. S. (1986). "Structure, Style, and Sense in Interpreting Thucydides: The Soldier's Choice (Thuc. 2.42.4)." *Harvard Studies in Classical Philology* 90: 49–76.

———. (1989). *Thucydides. The Peloponnesian War: Book II.* Cambridge.

Thomas, R. (1989). *Oral Tradition and Written Record in Classical Athens.* Cambridge.

Tritle, L. (2000). *From Melos to My Lai: War and Survival.* London.

Tyrrell, W. B. (1984). *Amazons. A Study in Athenian Mythmaking.* Baltimore.

Usher, S. (1999). *Greek Oratory. Tradition and Originality.* Oxford.

West, M. L. (1993). *Greek Lyric Poetry.* Oxford.

Wills, G. (1992). *Lincoln at Gettysburg: The Words That Remade America.* New York.

Ziolkowski, J. E. (1981). *Thucydides and the Tradition of Funeral Speeches at Athens.* Monographs in Classical Studies. New York.